Joan Kohn's

it's your bed and bath

Hundreds of Beautiful Design Ideas

Joan Kohn's

it's your bed and bath

Hundreds of Beautiful Design Ideas

bulfinch press

new york • boston

Bulfinch Press
Time Warner Book Group
1271 Avenue of the Americas
New York, NY 10020
Visit our Web site at www.bulfinchpress.com

First Edition

Library of Congress Cataloging-in-Publication Data
Kohn, Joan.
    [It's your bed and bath]
    Joan Kohn's it's your bed and bath : hundreds of beautiful design ideas / Joan Kohn. — 1st ed.
            p. cm.
Includes index.
    ISBN 0-8212-2831-5
    1. Bedrooms. 2. Bathrooms. 3. Interior decoration.   I. Title.
NK2117.B4K64 2004
747.7'7 — dc22   2003026619

Design by Lisa Vaughn-Soraghan, Two of Cups Design Studio

PRINTED IN SINGAPORE

To the sweet memory of my mother, Ruth, whose eye for beauty, persuasive wisdom, and hearty laughter are with me always, and to my father, Ned — the Chief — who built a sailboat, board by board, when he was only twelve, and years later taught us all to sail.

Acknowledgments

My most sincere gratitude to the artists — the architects, designers, and photographers — whose fine work appears in this book. I have the deepest respect for their extraordinary creativity, vitality, and zeal for beauty. In the course of our work, there have been many wonderful stories shared and many precious moments I shall never forget. I thank them all for these gifts.

Thanks also from the bottom of my heart to my dear friends and colleagues who have contributed so much to this book: to my fabulous editor at Bulfinch Press, Kristen Schilo, and to Jill Cohen, Karen Murgolo, Eveline Chao, Matthew Ballast, Jean Griffin, Adrienne Moucheraud, Alyn Evans, Peggy Leith Anderson, Barbara Nelson, and the rest of the Bulfinch team for their uncompromising pursuit of excellence; to Lisa Vaughn-Soraghan, the talented designer of this beautiful book, for her impeccable taste and sensitivity; to my wonderful literary agent, George Greenfield; to Ken Lowe, president and CEO of the The E. W. Scripps Company; to Burton Jablin, president of Home & Garden Television, and to Karen Wishart, Richard Grant, Freddy James, Dianne DiGregorio, Peter Clem, Jeana Niceley, Mike Boyd, Lori Calvert, Amy Gibson, and all my other friends at the network; to Peter Finn, executive producer of *Bed & Bath Design;* to Robert Stein, Denise Caplan, Oscar Alcantara, Alice Owings, and Michael Levy for their wise counsel; to publicist Maureen Legg of Legg Work, for all of her exceptional help; to Mike Strohl for introducing me to so many talented architects and designers; to my friend and colleague Judy Hedges for her keen eye and discerning insights; to Tom Connors and architect Michael Gelick for their thoughtful contributions; to Linda McClain and Bonnie Reddel for their guidance and good sense; to Taryn Kutchin and Penny Spentzas for their invaluable assistance and hard work; to my husband, Richard, for his love and support; and finally, to our mother, Adeline Kohn, whose sweetness, courage, and beauty are a constant inspiration.

contents

OPPOSITE
Design: Cullman and Kravis, Inc.

introduction

When I was a schoolgirl, a class in home economics was a standard part of a well-rounded curriculum. We baked oatmeal cookies, made our own aprons (each with a little pocket), hand-embroidered our names on gingham bags that held our supplies, and once in a while were even allowed to use the school's sewing machines. Back then the value of being a competent housekeeper was reinforced at home, where my mother drew constant delight from cleaning and "keeping things neat and orderly." Had her circumstances been different, she might have become an author herself, with *Zen and the Art of Ironing* as her first book. She regarded her daily chores as a privilege, and taught me the importance of caring graciously for family and friends. She also had a passion for good design. I love reminding my audiences to do something beautiful for themselves, because it allows me to pass along the essence of what my mother taught me, and because I think of her every time I say it.

My first design book, *It's Your Kitchen: Over 100 Inspirational Kitchens,* dealt with the busiest and most public space in today's home, the gathering place — *everyone's* room — where the design choices you make are strongly influenced by the impact they will have on others. But in this book, we turn to bedrooms and bathrooms: private rooms, where the forms, textures, and colors are devoted to serving your most intimate needs. Here the mood you set is just for you.

Fine design sustains and empowers us, refreshing and rekindling our life-spirit. Rooted in the wonder of nature's exquisite excess — interpreting her beauty and energy — it shelters and uplifts us. By harnessing the power of design, we enrich our lives every day. And nowhere is this impact more direct than in our bedrooms and bathrooms, the rooms devoted to refreshing our minds and our bodies, where we rest at night, then bathe and dress for a new day. Here, every design decision we make affects how we feel as we practice our most personal daily rituals. Every private room, whether drawn in serene simplicity or layers of pattern and personality, is a luxury. Some are upholstered in satin and silk; some are gilded; others define themselves with only the barest essentials. Each offers quietude.

This book is in two parts. Part one — "Design Essentials" — will help you understand the basic elements of bed and bath design, assess your existing rooms, make the most of your budget, gather inspiration, articulate your tastes, and assemble and work with a design team. In part two — "The Five Building Blocks of Bed and Bath Design" — we'll address the important issues of function, architecture, floor plan, style, and personal touch.

Illustrated with photographs taken by many of the world's finest architectural photographers and representing the work of top architects and designers, this book covers a wide array of traditional and contemporary design styles. Each was selected to represent bed and bath design at its best, and intended to provide you with useful ideas that you can adapt to suit your life, your style, and your budget — to spark your imagination as you design beautiful rooms of your very own.

By approaching the bed and bath design process from conception to completion, the methods presented here (which apply to any project, from a modest powder room makeover to a grand master suite addition) will teach your how to achieve your goals with clarity and self-confidence.

prelude: nantucket powder room with pitcher

"This place is just magic." Architect Lyman Perry was exhilarated, a bit out of breath, and very happy to be docked safely in Nantucket harbor when I reached him on his cell phone. His early sail had been rough; the winds were strong, and getting into harbor had required some strenuous tacking. "I'm here on the pier," he said. "I just sailed up — let me get out of the wind — but I can talk now."

Although I was reluctant at first to draw him away from the fullness of that glorious private moment, I quickly realized Lyman's passions for sailing, for Nantucket, and for architecture were so intertwined that this might not be an interruption at all. In fact, the timing seemed to be perfect. After all, in architecture and design, context is everything.

Lyman called Nantucket a jewel. He compared it to a ship anchored thirty miles from shore, wrapped in the icy waters that flow down from Nova Scotia. Sometimes called the Gray Lady, this morning she was all a-sparkle, dazzlingly alive and alert. Lyman spoke in detail about the winds — how quickly they can toss aside the gray island mists, and how they carry the heavy smells of the beach and the moors. Nantucket has an English landscape and, of course, a nautical heritage. Descended from an illustrious line of navy men, Lyman finds it all bracing and invigorating.

It was here, amidst this natural splendor, that he had worked with interior designer Trudy Dujardin, a longtime collaborator, on her own Nantucket home. The powder room, but a fraction of a tireless, two-year project, is itself a jewel, representing well the vision they set out to achieve.

In sharp contrast to the main entry hall with its vivacious views of the ever-changing harbor, the powder room offers family and friends a private moment of welcome. It is a small, quiet room set at the end of a 6-foot corridor lined with a coat closet on one side and an antique hall table on the other.

As its door opens, we are at once embraced by the warmth and generosity of Trudy's spirit, as well as by her love of this island and its people. The washstand — retrieved from the home of an old sea captain, then refinished — is appointed with a Dresden china pitcher and bowl (a gift from Trudy's mother), a tiny silver box, and fine hand-embroidered Irish linens, and accented by an old sepia photograph of several young Nantucket sailors, all bursting with smiles and laughter. Above the photograph is a vintage mirror that Trudy "had to have." More island memorabilia, collected over many years, adorn the walls of this precious inner sanctum. And through the powder room window, a lovely flower garden slopes gently upward to best display its profusion of blooms.

Like so many great designs, this powder room breathes in the surrounding beauty, then graciously exhales it back into the environment for all of us to savor. As if by means of some mysterious design photosynthesis, it seems to make the air even richer. In Trudy's home this is quite literally the case; because of her commitment to healthy building practices, everything is environmentally sensitive and nontoxic.

Artistry, Honesty, Serenity, Strength . . . There is heart and history in each well-chosen detail, making this a perfect place from which to begin our study of bedrooms and baths.

part one:

design essentials

Vision is a postcard and a road map, a combination of wonder and wisdom that brings you safely to your design destination.

ABOVE Soft textiles and gentle light combine to create a comfortable corner for reading and rest.

OPPOSITE Layers of linens cascade sensuously onto the floor, and all is arranged for long hours of quiet escape in this bedroom drawn with clean lines and sandy hues.
Design: Clodagh

every room has a personality. How do you imagine yours? Is it a graceful space that expresses itself in whispers, or an energetic room with strong opinions? Does it gaze back in time or look ahead? Has it traveled to romantic places and developed an appetite for antiquities or exotic textiles? Perhaps its tastes are simple. Is this a room that changes its mind, or one that holds on to the tried-and-true? Does it welcome houseguests or is it meant for you alone?

Does your room wear slippers or go barefoot? Does it let you throw your socks on the floor, or insist that you use the hamper? Is it casual enough to let you leave the bed unmade all day in case you decide to take an afternoon nap? Or is it formal and grand, with an elegance that provides its own luxurious comfort? Does it feel like *your* room? Does it make you smile?

one
vision

Classic order and
symmetry are the hallmarks of
this pure white New England
master bathroom. Sensitively
proportioned, with attention to
each understated detail, it has a
stature beyond its modest scale.
Design: Sally Weston

Great designs begin with a clear and specific
vision — a core idea that will energize and sustain you
throughout the long process ahead. The more precisely you are
able to see yourself bathing, dressing, and sleeping in your new
bath or bedroom, the greater your chance of building rooms
that work well for you. Your vision will inspire you, guide you
through the maze of design choices ahead, and help you
maintain your composure when the wrong bathroom tile is
delivered for the third time or your contractor announces that
he'll be dog-sledding in Alaska for the month of March.

Creating your vision is a two-step process. Step one is to
allow your dreams to run wild — without boundaries or
budgets — picking up ideas from every possible source. Step
two involves refining those dreams in light of more practical
considerations, such as the square footage and configuration of
your available space, your specific functional needs, and your
resources. Like a string on a kite, these considerations will
prevent your dream from soaring out of sight.

Step One: Spinning Bed and Bath Dreams

Conjuring up dreams of your new bedroom or bathroom
begins with one essential question: How do you envision life
in your new room?

➤ Can you imagine a perfect spot that makes you feel it's
just where you belong? What are you doing there —
resting, reading, playing a board game, doing a jigsaw
puzzle? What are you wearing? Is there anything to eat?
Are you listening to music? What are the other sounds
you hear? Is there fragrance in the air?

➤ On Sunday mornings, are you lounging in bed with a cup
of coffee and a newspaper? Or is the whole family gathered around, watching TV?

➤ Is this a room you're planning to enjoy forever, or will you
be moving in a few years?

Practice mentally bringing your rooms to life. Athletes, astronauts, and actors are taught to reinforce their training with precise mental visualizations. Designers and architects do the same thing, and so should you. Envisioning success leads to success. Draw, daydream, or lull yourself to sleep at night by walking through your new rooms, arranging the furniture, and organizing your new closet. The ability to imagine yourself there, with everything just as you like it, is true vision.

ABOVE AND RIGHT Referencing the historical Southwest, this vision balances dark woodwork and furniture with creamy Venetian plaster walls, columns, and textiles. The classic arch motif is woven through both the architecture and the interior design.
Design: Morehouse MacDonald and Associates, Inc.

As you visualize your new bed and bath, remember these three rules:

First, in these all-important private spaces, away from the rest of the world, your dreams must be your own — not your best friend's, not your neighbor's, not even your mother's. It's *your* bed and bath . . . design it that way!

Second, your dreams should be sweet. Creativity calls for freedom and flights of fancy. Dream wide and dream big.

Third, don't rush the process. Schedules and deadlines will confront you soon enough. For now, savor the luxury of time. What may seem like an indulgence is actually the wisest investment you can make in your project. The more deliberately and specifically you plan today, the greater your rewards are sure to be.

If your bed and bath ideas are not fully formed, you can stimulate your imagination in many ways. One obvious way is to collect ideas from pictures in magazines and books — not to mention your favorite TV shows! — using the techniques discussed in chapter five. Or perhaps the beds, bathtubs, and showers presented in chapter six will help you recognize your dream when you *feel* it.

And there are other great ways to spark your imagination:

➢ Use the suggestions in chapter eight to help you analyze why you want a new bed or bath, and how you want to use it.

➢ Decide what you like and do not like about your existing bed and bath. Chapter three will help you with this process.

➢ Throughout it all, keep a detailed written wish list chronicling your thoughts as they occur to you.

OPPOSITE Like brushstrokes of Asian calligraphy, this design draws power from its confident simplicity. To underscore the strong geometry of this vision, the architects chose a mild and uniform palette with a floor of honed white limestone, walls finished with satin titanium paint, a marble trough sink set on stainless steel legs, and glass walls framed in steel.
Design: Gabellini Associates

RIGHT With the flick of a switch, milky white walls of low-voltage privacy glass theatrically become window walls, providing a clear view into the bedroom.
Design: Gabellini Associates

Step Two: Refining Your Bed and Bath Dreams

The process of refining a dream is as important as the dream itself. For true success, every design must accommodate practical realities. Some adjustments are always necessary. Focus on how you can maintain the *essence* of your dream — the core idea that will have the most impact — even if on a modest scale. Selectivity is the key. Homeowners are often surprised to discover how an apparent compromise can take their design in a wonderful, unexpected direction.

From time to time, a design vision may spring from a sudden burst of inspiration. But don't count on that proverbial lightbulb going on. It is far more likely that your vision will evolve slowly and painstakingly, the result of thoughtful preparation.

When facing a wide array of design choices, expect to feel a bit overwhelmed. But, as with unwinding a spool of thread, the trick is in getting started, in finding that little notch that holds the thread. Your first decision will lead to the next, and soon your design will begin rolling out before your eyes in a logical and easy way.

LEFT This master suite, inspired by New England barn architecture, is a new addition to a low and rambling Cape Cod–style house. The suite was purposely mismatched with the rest of the home to add character and timeworn appeal. The homeowners had always envisioned sleeping under the handsome timbers of a high-pitched roof, and built the addition to accommodate both a sleeping area and a private entertainment area.
Design: Duckham + McDougal Architects

RIGHT Fearless of heights, this master bedroom is a bold and confident vision.
Design: Roger Bellera

BELOW With youthful freedom and visionary irreverence, this sleeping loft recycles raw materials that might otherwise have been discarded and invents a new urban aesthetic, a new economy, and a new way to find beauty.
Design: LOT/EK

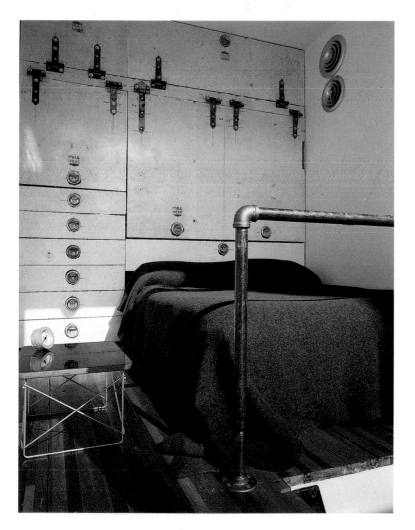

Thinking About Resale

Today, prospective home buyers looking beyond necessity and toward a sense of personal luxury pay particular attention to bathrooms, where so many of the design choices become a permanent part of the architecture. Therefore, if maximizing the resale value of your home is important to you, remember that it is always safer to select bathroom fixtures and materials that are consistent with more than one style, allowing buyers to readily imagine adapting your space to their own needs and personal tastes. Realtors may call white the color for resale, but you do not have to sacrifice your preferences to make your home more marketable, so long as your choices are gracefully neutral and harmonious. If you have a passion for intense color and exotic patterns, think about channeling those impulses into the choices you make for the wall colors, textiles, accessories, and other elements that can easily be changed by a new owner.

LEFT AND ABOVE This large-scale master bedroom, with an adjoining bath, is subtly divided into separate sleeping and entertainment areas. Lush furnishings and textiles enjoy the twin luxuries of ample space and glorious natural light.
Design: Scott Himmel, Architect P.C.

**Here are a few more special rooms filled with
ideas to get you dreaming . . .**

Architect Scott Himmel understands the importance of
making an entrance. The regal proportions of this 60-foot-
long bedroom entry corridor are enhanced by natural daylight,
which pours through an extraordinary skylight designed by
architect Samuel Marx in the late 1920s. Just above the sandblasted glass sits an empty 8 x 60-foot space built for the sole
purpose of collecting light from above. A French-wool runner
in a delicate floral pattern and gilded Venetian antiques lead us
into the master bedroom, where we are once again bathed in

light. Three sets of double French doors, an angled ceiling
(designed to match the dormers of the mansard roofline), and
a fireplace provide the architectural framework that inspired
this vision. Rooted in neoclassic traditions, the design draws
from Asia and America as well. An eighteenth-century hand-
carved French commode is paired with a black-and-gold
Chinese screen and cabinet. Cream-colored fabrics and wall-
to-wall carpeting harmonize with fabric-paneled walls in a
muted-peach, tea-dyed floral pattern. White and aqua bed
linens under a mushroom-toned linen velvet headboard
complete this well-balanced and stately picture.

OPPOSITE, LEFT, AND BELOW
A vaulted ceiling, fabricated
of high-tech materials, borrows
its form from the gently
overarching canopy of trees in
the surrounding landscape.
Design: Sura Malaga-Strachan

This master suite began with a minimalist photo
that two young homeowners had torn from a design magazine.
In a new home built far from the busy city on ten acres of
farmland, their goal was tranquillity. After a few weeks
of conversation and some preliminary sketches, the couple
decided upon this unique combination of natural and synthetic
materials. Unfettered by any single design tradition, it
expresses daring ideas that are both organic and industrial.
A built-in maple vanity on one side of the bathroom opposes
a sculpted steel pedestal sink under a ribbon of windows.
Some pieces float free of the wall, while others are anchored
to it. Soft curves, creamy limestone, marble conglomerate,
warm wood floors, and muted green on the walls and in the
textiles add subtle variety, yet provide a dramatic contrast to
the corrugated steel roof and its heavy iron trusses, the
exposed ductwork, and the abstract floor plan. The entry
hall, itself a dramatic sculptural form, accommodates a
growing art collection.

And here's another surprise: The "ballet bar" in the
bedroom was actually built to hold the bedspread at night!

Ignited by the vibrant enthusiasm of their clients and generously graced with total creative freedom, Jean Verbridge and Thad Siemasko designed this unique master suite to soak up the vast views of the Atlantic. Wanting to live as close to the outdoors as possible, the homeowners envisioned a master suite where they were enveloped by the panorama. A wide-open sense of blue sky and water is balanced by the sheltering power of the architecture. While simple lines and a neutral palette allow nature to take center stage, the dramatic structure of the ceilings and vast expanses of glass heighten the experience of every morning sunrise and every ocean storm.

As in so many successful collaborations, there was a high level of understanding between the designers and their clients.

Mutual trust became a powerful source of creative energy, making hard work feel like play, and generating a design that gave the owners the precise feeling they wanted, but in an utterly fresh style.

Final Thoughts

Some design visions will be born from a moment's inspiration. Others will occur effortlessly and naturally over time or make themselves known only after a battle of fits and starts. But at its core, every design vision is born from something simple inside you that responds to something simple from the world: a color, a touch, a scent, a feeling, a memory — that essential connection that resonates within you, and somehow expresses who you are.

OPPOSITE AND RIGHT Creating the illusion of a 360-degree view, this striking architecture takes in the Atlantic Ocean with curved walls of windows as sky pours in from a domed ceiling high over the master bed and from an arched window above the tub.
Design: Jean Verbridge and Thaddeus Siemasko

The elements of design are fixed and few, but in combination they make anything possible.

1ike all fine works of art and architecture, beautiful bedrooms and baths have a power to evoke a strong emotional response in each of us. Yet it is important to remember that just as every great novel is made up of letters of the alphabet, and symphonies are arrangements of notes, all well-designed rooms — however grand or modest — are composed of the very same fundamental elements of design: line, texture, color, mass, harmony, contrast, and balance.

Learning to recognize these elements and how they work together in a successful design will enable you to better understand and communicate your personal aesthetic, extracting the essence of what you love about any beautiful room and putting it to work in your own home.

ABOVE AND OPPOSITE Lines create rhythms and patterns that define the style and mood of your rooms.
Design: Andre Rothblatt

two

the elements of bed & bath design

LEFT The curved lines of a slipper tub on claw feet set a soft, traditional tone.
Design: Matthew Patrick Smyth

OPPOSITE In this contemporary design, bold rectilinear lines are accented by the wavelike interior of the tub.
Design: Marmol Radziner + Associates and Monica Conroy Bodell

Line

Line is the most basic element of design, defining style as it glides, darts, curls, swerves, angles, wanders, and zigzags through a space, forming walls, ceilings, floors, and furnishings. Generally, traditional styles are characterized by more curved and ornamented lines, while contemporary styles often employ lines that are straighter and less embellished.

Because of their inherent emotional power — thick lines feel strong, thin lines are delicate, angles are energetic — lines combine in an endless profusion of rhythms and patterns that can alter our thoughts and feelings as we enter a room. The lines in a French country bedroom may embrace us with their warmth and comfort, while an Asian minimalist bathroom can offer a cool serenity.

Texture

The most sensuous element of design is texture. Appealing to
our touch as well as our sight, the textures we feel also make *us*
feel. Satin-finished stainless steel can cool down a design;
plush fabrics quickly warm it up. By opposing rough surfaces
against smooth, hard against soft, heavy against light, natural
against synthetic, patterned against plain, and reflective against
matte, we can enrich any room.

Texture can enter unobtrusively or with a splash. It can be
embossed onto tiles or towels, gently veined into marble, or
woven into textiles. It can be molded, seeded, pressed, stained,
ribbed, or fused into glass. Woods are grained, granite is
dappled. Concrete can be polished or rough, copper mottled,
laminates patterned. Metals can be coarse or smooth, shiny or
dull. Terry cloth is warm and fuzzy, satin slippery.

Color

More than any other element of design, color creates mood. In its infinite variety, color can soothe or shake, relax or enliven, dazzle or lull. It can be warm, spirited, and embracing, or cool, calm, and collected. Mutable and ever-shifting, responsive and sensitive, color is changed by alterations in natural and artificial light and by the colors, materials, and textures with which it is paired.

When color is bold and brash it confronts and disarms us, taking command of a design. When it is soft and mysterious, it persuades us gently.

There are endless ways for you to explore the creative potential of your favorite color. Let it shimmer through tiles of glass or watch it glow from under a glaze of bronze. Gray it down, fleck it with gold, shade it, tint it, or give it a chalky feel. Let it run wild in veins of marble, or tame it under veils of gauze and chiffon.

Color captivates and stimulates us from the moment of birth. It has the power to change our mood and even our appetite. It insinuates itself into our dreams. Surely there is no better place to surround ourselves with the colors that move us than in our most private rooms.

LEFT Intense color can dominate even the strongest architectural elements.
Design: Carl D'Aquino, Francine Monaco, and Paul Laird

ABOVE Every decision you make about materials is a color choice as well. Even glass and metals come in many different hues.
Design: Scott Himmel, Architect P.C.

RIGHT Neutrals, alone or in combination, also add color to a design.
Design: Brininstool + Lynch

Mass

You can paint a perfect picture using lines, textures, and colors,
but to design a room, you must think in three dimensions.
Mass begins with line, but as that line moves into space, everything changes. Rectangles sketched on paper become bathtubs,
dressers, and beds — objects with heft, depth, and height.

Evaluate positive masses (like the bed) and negative
spaces (open areas, empty recesses, nooks, and corridors) for
both utility and beauty. Bedrooms and bathrooms must be
sculpted, and the goal is always to find a proper balance —
one that allows you to move in and through your rooms with
comfort and ease.

Scale

A delicate and ephemeral sense of rightness is the hallmark of all well-proportioned rooms. Entryways relate to the size of the rooms, nightstands to the bed, faucets to the sink, the graining of the marble to the size of the slab. Achieving just the right relationships between all the architectural and interior elements is rarely a matter of guesswork; it requires careful observation and a certain measure of experimentation. While good proportions are quite apt to go unnoticed, the results can be disastrous if they are flawed.

Harmony, Contrast, and Balance

In our tantalizing and often frustrating creative struggles to piece together just the right lines, colors, textures, and shapes, there is no known guaranteed formula for success — not even from the richest, rarest, most sought-after materials. What is certain is that all good design expresses an effortless compatibility among its component parts. This agreeable harmony is then complemented, refreshed, and enlightened by notes of contrast that keep it fresh and alive. Combining the visual and tactile, the overt and the understated, the concrete and the subconscious, every good design finds balance. In bed and bath design the result is the creation of a world complete and whole, offering a seamless, uninterrupted sense of place and peace.

Yet designs that rise to the realm of greatness are apt to include two more elements: clarity and restraint.

RIGHT The softly curving lines of this vintage tub, complemented by stained-glass peonies and Calcutta marble, set a charming, traditional tone.
Design: Stuart Cohen & Julie Hacker Architects

OPPOSITE At once cozy and wide open, this classic white bathroom is replete with delicate contrasts and captivating details.
Design: Stuart Cohen & Julie Hacker Architects

Clarity

Clarity is honesty delivered with directness. Your private rooms can tell whatever story you want to tell in the lovely, wordless language of color, texture, and form. The more authentic the story — the closer it comes to revealing who you are — the more successful your design will be. Yours may be a story that began in childhood, about family history and friends, or your story may simply be about quiet and rest. Your design may be about sustaining our planet or about venturing around it. Whether your rooms are plain or fancy, classic or inventive, put truth into every detail.

Restraint

There is one small but potent danger in the intoxicating effect of beauty. As experienced artists and artisans will tell you, one of the most difficult lessons to learn is when a piece of work is complete. Beware the danger of too many good ideas, of too many embellishments, and even of too much design.

Final Thoughts

There is a spherical quality to good design — a sense of completeness. With no apparent beginning or end, the best designs seem to feel just right. They belong, they fit; and when they do, we are all captivated by their impact.

The rooms you presently live in hold secrets for your future design success.

ABOVE Mirrored walls double the light, while antique linens and heirlooms add a sense of history. Additional space for this room was borrowed from closets in the bedroom.

OPPOSITE A pink-and-cream canopy framed with crown molding creates a chamber-within-the-bedchamber, adding stature to a small space.
Design: Whitney Stewart Interior Design

taking a close — even microscopic — look at your existing bedroom and bath will provide you with essential design clues for your new project. Careful analysis of your personal habits and daily routines will reveal the key patterns and well-worn paths of your life, details critical to your decisions about what must stay and what must go. Starting over does not necessarily mean starting from scratch. If you're building a new home or addition, there's a good chance you'll want to bring some of your past along with you, and if you're remodeling, it makes sense to take advantage of what you already have.

This chapter includes a "tool kit" and a questionnaire to help you harness your creativity when assessing your existing bed and bath, as well as examples of creative problem solving by homeowners intent upon making the most of what they had.

three

assessing your existing bed & bath

Joan's Tool Kit

The nuts and bolts of this tool kit are not standard issue. You won't find any screwdrivers, hammers, or nails. Instead, you'll find tools necessary to maximize your creativity and improve your ability to observe and communicate. These tools will help you solve problems and deal with design challenges and construction frustrations as they come up — or maybe even before they do.

For order and convenience, keep your tools together. A tote of any kind will do the job: a mesh gardening bag, a plumber's satchel, a basket, or even a briefcase. Set the right standard for your design project by choosing something that's as pleasant to look at and carry as it is convenient to use. Then fill it with these basic items:

A Camera

Good ideas pop up suddenly and unexpectedly. So get the lightest and most compact camera you can, one that you can take with you wherever you go. Having a simple means of capturing ideas for future reference is a big practical advantage. Your camera eliminates the pressure of having to remember everything you see. And while you may never forget that fabulous hotel suite in Charleston where you stayed on your honeymoon, your camera will retain all the specifics, such as the mirrored panels above the bathroom tile or the practical little kitchenette built into a corner of the walk-in closet. Specifics make a huge design difference!

Your camera also helps you become a design detective during the assessment and evaluation stage of your project. By employing its impartial lens, you will see the realities of your room. Unlike most of us, the camera does not see only what it wants to see. It won't overlook the peeling paint on the ceiling of the shower, or ignore that ragtag nest of knotted wires on the floor next to the bed. If you're feeling courageous, let your camera have a peek into your medicine cabinet and dresser drawers too! The camera's eye will train your own eyes to be objective, helping you to become more discerning and improving your ability to refine and edit your design decisions.

A Tape Recorder

Your tape recorder will make you a better listener, helping you serve the needs of the people with whom you will share your new rooms. Ask them to answer thoughtfully the same kinds of lifestyle and aesthetic questions you ask yourself. The conversations you save on your tape recorder can have a significant impact on your plans. Listening, like seeing, can quickly become a selective process, because it is always easier to hear only what we want to hear. Learning that your spouse or partner no longer likes highly saturated colors or has a long-standing wish for a steam shower is important information. Careful listening simplifies decision making.

Yellow Sticky Notes

These little guys can be a big help as you prepare your wish list. Using them couldn't be simpler. Every time you notice a problem in one of your existing rooms, take a moment to jot it on a little sticky, then paste it directly on the offending spot. Are your closets overcrowded? Mark them yellow. Is the shower too small or the tub too large? Slap on a sticky. That slow leak under the vanity? Give it the yellow badge of discouragement. Once a room looks like a bowl of lemons, it's time to remodel.

A Measuring Tape

To ensure that all your ideas, furniture, and fixtures will fit into your new room, include a tape measure in your tool kit. Proper proportions and a good fit are an absolute necessity from floor to ceiling. Professional carpenters say, "Measure twice, cut once." This is a good rule to follow as you connect all the dots of your design puzzle. No aspect of design should be a guessing game. When in doubt, measure three times.

An Address Book / Calendar

Keeping your paperwork accurate and orderly is a must. Even more important is having an organized list of correct names, addresses, telephone and fax numbers, and e-mail addresses. An even higher priority is getting to know the people who will be on your design team — understanding their work habits and finding convenient and comfortable ways to communicate with them.

Unless you have a photographic memory or exceptional "people skills," you will need to write down the details — *all* of them. Do your best to remember names: not just of your contractor, painter, or the salesperson at your favorite tile store, but of assistants and office managers as well. This is a gracious first step toward establishing good long-term relationships.

The calendar is important for scheduling work, arranging deliveries, and keeping appointments. It's also the best place to maintain a running list of the agreements and arrangements that you've made with workers and others. Daily jottings on your calendar that include names and specific notes of conversations and of promises made are a practical and easy way to keep chaos and mental confusion to a minimum.

A Receipts File

A file dedicated to receipts and bills will help you monitor and assess the many financial aspects of your project. Knowing where you stand financially is crucial to completing your job in style. No matter how luxurious your new bedroom may be, you won't sleep comfortably there if you've gone too far above budget. Balance is the hallmark of good design, not only aesthetically but financially as well.

A Hand Mirror

Self-knowledge is the key to design success. Use this tool to look yourself squarely in the eye. It will help you answer honestly the preparatory questionnaire on pages 51–53 and enable you to set appropriate goals and make strong decisions. This mirror is a symbol of yourself, serving as a reminder of your importance to your entire design team.

A Journal

Designing, building, and remodeling is a big deal! It will monopolize your time, energy, creativity, right brain, left brain, and virtually all your resources for a long time. A good way to collect your thoughts is to keep a journal. It makes sense to follow the example of artists and leaders in all fields who have successfully employed this time-tested method of self-exploration. A fifteen-minute investment every day — for me, morning is best — will pay you back with more than just

penmanship practice. A journal is like a new best friend. Happy to hear all your excitement and complaints, it can provide you with wonderful new insights. Record new ideas, express your joys, vent your tensions and fears, and grapple with your problems. You don't have to be right or wrong. You can babble. You can brag. Whining on occasion is okay too.

ABOVE With careful assessment, neglected space under an eave becomes a charming focal point.
Design: Joan Dineen

RIGHT One big challenge was finding room for a second sink; this highly inventive solution was born of necessity.
Design: Joan Halperin/Interior Design

BELOW The once-trendy turquoise tiles and sink and the geometric wallpaper "had to go." And the two tiers of café curtains above the rather elaborate vanity table and stool recalled a bygone era that the homeowners preferred to keep only as a memory.

Before . . . and After

The problem: There was too little space in a 1950s ranch house for the contemporary needs of two busy professionals, each wanting better function and ample storage space. The solution: Avoid major exterior architectural reconstruction by using glass walls to visually open the corner shower, install a step to the newly sunken tub, then float a second vanity and telescoping mirror over its edge, creating an interlocking grid of highly efficient sculpted forms. Sheathed in handsome green marble that unifies the design, the bold, monolithic geometry of these surfaces creates an up-to-date sophistication that suits these homeowners perfectly.

Because bedrooms and bathrooms have such a
high priority in our lives today, architects and designers must
consistently find practical ways to maximize their size, function, and aesthetic potential. In a vintage residence in Chicago
(shown below and right), four separate spaces with varying
ceiling heights and flooring materials have been united to
create one spacious master bathroom. A newly installed
skylight compensates for the lack of natural light, and an
antique tub, authentic period-style tile, and woodwork
inspired by the home's original detailing complete the effect.

In a New York City condominium (shown opposite), the
existing 8-foot ceilings presented a challenge when trying to
create an elegant, old-world aesthetic. In order to create the
effect of a higher ceiling, custom-detailed cabinetry was
constructed with doors that reach the new crown molding.

These built-ins also provide much-needed storage and define
an illuminated niche that holds the rare antique commode. In
addition, the drapery hardware was neatly concealed behind
the crown molding, so that the lean line of the drapery panels
is not interrupted. The opulence of the Louis XVI gilded bed
is balanced by a harmonious envelope of soft, creamy linens
and silks. Wall-to-wall carpeting also unifies the floor plane,
further maximizing the sense of space.

OPPOSITE Subtle architectural
changes transformed a boxlike room in a modern high-rise
apartment building into an
elegant master suite worthy
of its furnishings.
Design: Sabrina Balsky Interior Design Inc.

ABOVE AND LEFT This
accommodating, spacious, and
well-lit renovated bathroom was
designed to look as if it had been
here since the Roaring Twenties,
when the home was originally built.
Design: Christine Julian and
Lynn Aseltine-Kolbusz

In the bathroom shown above, a rectangular, windowless space in a new building was magically transformed into a luminous and dramatic oval of shimmering white marble. On the floor, a spoke pattern of black and green marble mosaic reinforces the curvilinear shape of the space. Lean, black columns on delicate pedestals lead the eye to the oval cove of light above, adorned with a 1940s Italian chandelier of amber-tinted glass and silver. White lacquer, crystal, nickel, and exquisite personal accessories complete the mood of glamour and luxury. The simple sycamore chair upholstered in terry cloth was designed for the famous French ocean liner *Normandie*, the heavy base keeping the chair steady as the ship sailed over choppy seas. This bathroom is a truly miraculous example of what can happen when a designer and his clients are simply unwilling to allow their vision to be compromised by the limitations of an existing space.

Assessing Your Design Needs

Answering these questions will help you analyze how your bed and bath should look and feel:

Part 1. Lifestyle and Aesthetics

➤ On a scale of 1–10, how beautiful — and how comfortable — are your rooms?

➤ How often do you find yourself yearning for a new bedroom or bath?

➤ Have your personal or family needs changed over the years? Do you expect changes ahead?

➤ Do you have a favorite spot in the bedroom — a perfect place to read or work?

➤ What are the "must-haves" for your new design?

➤ What was the worst mistake made in the design of your present bedroom or bathroom? Is there something that annoys you, or that you've had to learn to live with?

➤ What's your immediate reaction to the bedroom when you open your eyes in the morning?

➤ Is there enough space, seating, and storage for everyone to be comfortable?

➤ What are your sleeping habits? Can you bathe, groom, and dress without disturbing your partner?

➤ Does anyone have disabilities or other special needs that require adjustments to your design?

➤ Is there a family pet to accommodate, perhaps with a sleeping area?

➤ Do you wish to expand the function of your room? Perhaps you'd like an entertainment or exercise area, a desk space, a small snacking kitchen, a sauna, or access to the outdoors.

➤ Is there too much of your past in the decor and not enough of your future?

➤ Ranking the rooms in your house in order of preference, how high on the list is this room? What characteristics of your favorite room might be transferred successfully to your new bedroom or bath design?

Part 2. The Space

➤ Have you examined every elevation of the room — the walls, ceiling, and floor — to look for ways to improve the space? Are doors and windows well placed? How might you enhance the architectural shell with minor or major changes?

➤ Are there opportunities for expanding your existing space, such as an empty corner or an unused area under a stairwell? Is there an adjacent attic, basement, hallway, closet, or spare room from which to borrow some extra space? How about adding a dormer?

➤ If the available space is ample, how might it best be partitioned or otherwise segmented into distinct functional areas?

➤ How's the traffic pattern inside the room? Can you move around and through the space with ease, or do you find yourself bumping into objects or people?

➤ How about the traffic flow between rooms? And does your room have a gracious entry?

➤ How easy is it to make your bed? Where do you place your bedcovers at night?

➤ Is the bedroom dark enough for sleeping? Does the lighting plan balance natural with artificial light and provide good general, task, and accent lighting? Does the room enjoy enough sunshine? Are light switches conveniently located?

- Is your bedroom quiet enough for sleep and relaxation?

- Are your rooms wired to accommodate all necessary equipment and technology?

- What is the room's relationship to the out-of-doors? Is there a way to improve it, with new windows, doors, skylights, or perhaps a new patio or balcony?

- Do you have enough space to fill all your storage needs? Can you readily find what you're looking for, or do you rummage and hunt? Are there items you've stored in the attic or basement that you wish you could use regularly?

- When cleaning your closet, do you find things you didn't remember you had?

- Do you have adequate places to display your decorative pieces, family treasures, and art?

ABOVE Simple architectural details, including shutters, shelves, and a handsome tub enclosure, add style, storage, and stature to this small bathroom.
Design: Sally Weston

LEFT With a vivid imagination, a tiny trapezoid was transformed into an enchanting bedroom filled with sunshine, storage, and even a small sink.
Design: Ivan Bercedo and Jorge Mestre

Part 3. Condition

➢ What is the current condition of your room — including floors, ceilings, finishes, walls, and trim? Are the doors and windows in good shape?

➢ Are your fixtures in good working order? Does the interior hardware on your cabinetry work well? Do the doors and drawers open and close smoothly?

➢ Are the heating and air-conditioning in good repair? Is the level of humidity appropriate?

➢ How much time do you spend taking care of this room? Is maintenance overly burdensome? What chore would you most like to eliminate?

➢ Do you understand all the pros and cons of any new materials you're considering for your new design? For example, will that new vanity top you want require periodic sealing to avoid stains?

Final Thoughts

The relationship you have with your bedrooms and baths is personal and private. You are the only one who knows all the important questions that must be answered before you finalize your design plans. A careful examination of your rooms and everything in them will help ensure that your new rooms will work beautifully for you.

RIGHT Two sheets of glass lined with glimmering rice paper allow natural light to flow into a windowless interior bathroom. Glass panels are also used to construct the sink, shower, and even the bathtub beyond, further enhancing the sparkle.
Design: Joan Dineen

As your design dreams collide with reality, expect creative sparks to fly.

Your vision may be ideal, but bringing it to life will be a problem-solving, labor-intensive process. Limitations of space, light, money, and even time and energy will affect every design choice you make. Happily, serious struggles with hard realities often result in inventive solutions and unimagined success.

Every design professional faces the challenge of how to use money wisely and well. Often, the grander the project, the greater the need for shrewd spending. And most projects — even those that appear to have had no restrictions at all — incorporate clever economies that we can borrow and adapt in precisely the same way we borrow and adapt their glorious design ideas.

four

budgeting your resources

Balance is the key to beauty as well as budget.
Although there is an undeniable power in precious materials
such as marble, granite, exotic woods, gold leaf, and molded
or carved plaster, all good design is rooted in proportion and
balance. One sure path to success is to adapt the essentials of
your chosen aesthetic to the scale of your project, interpreting
its lines, patterns, colors, and spirit in affordable materials.

In the exquisitely refined bathroom shown above and
right, the glass door and walls, soaking tub and sink, hardware,
and faucets were all custom-designed and fabricated at great
expense. The bathroom shown opposite — designed by the
same architect and inspired by the same Japanese aesthetic —
relies on standard fixtures and far less expensive materials.
Yet these two rooms share many common design features.
Both rely on the repetition of rectilinear forms. Both employ
a restrained, neutral palette and minimalist hardware. And

OPPOSITE With absolute purity of form, this serene aesthetic is meticulously expressed in the richest raw materials: maple-stained mahogany, limestone slabs, and sandblasted glass.
Design: Brininstool + Lynch

RIGHT The Asian aesthetic can also be realized in affordable cinder block, plywood, and ceramic tile, with accents of slate.
Design: Brininstool + Lynch

both use translucent panels to gather light and impart a magical luminescence: walls and a door of sandblasted glass in the more expensive room, and a polycarbonate faux window above the tub in our more affordable example. In both of these bathrooms, the art is in the architecture.

Ideas to Help You Stay On Budget

➤ **Invest in permanence.** The money you spend on architecture will reap great dividends. While furniture, fabrics, and accessories can be upgraded later, the architecture will endure, providing the framework for your bedroom or bathroom design. If you're not ready to invest in extensive exterior or interior renovations, consider smaller, more cost-efficient architectural upgrades. Install crown moldings or rosettes on the ceiling or chair rails on the walls, add pilasters in a doorcase, support a shelf or

mantel with corbels, define new spaces with cabinetry, or create a niche, nook, or archway. Sometimes turning a window into a doorway (efficient because less reconstruction is needed) transforms the relationship between your suite and a porch, patio, or garden.

➤ If you're living in a rental space, investing in permanence may mean putting your money into fine furnishings and other items that you can take with you when you move. For example, if you love stained glass, a removable stained-glass panel hanging in front of a window may be a better choice than a permanently installed window.

➤ **Find hidden treasures.** Salvaged or found objects can enrich your rooms; their aged patina can contribute a new look. Unusual objects, such as street signs or architectural fragments taken out of their usual context, can add an energetic jolt to your design. And don't forget to shop at home . . . literally! Your basement, attic, living room, or entry hall may be holding hidden treasures that truly belong in the new master bath.

➤ **Create one focal point.** Focus your investment where it will have the biggest impact. In most rooms, the need for beauty is readily satisfied with a single, well-conceived focal point, allowing you to complete your design with more modestly priced materials, such as standard 4 x 4-inch ceramic field tiles and bead board, without any loss of style.

➤ **For an upscale look, scale down.** The big advantage of small spaces is that they require fewer yards of fabric, gallons of paint, and square feet of tile. So instead of spending your money on building larger rooms than you

need or will use, build smaller rooms and invest your money in making them as perfect as possible.

Pare down the number of unused objects in your life. (Here's a tip for getting a fresh start in your new room: Saying good-bye to objects with sentimental value, from small mementos to large pieces of furniture, can be difficult. Consider saving them in a memory book, with snapshots and stories of the memories they hold; then pass the objects themselves along to a friend, relative, or worthy charity where they can find a new home.)

> **Monitor your momentum.** As the design process moves forward, it's easy to get carried away. Excitement at the sight of something new or extraordinary in a store, combined with our natural desire to finish the design project, can cause us to make too many choices too soon. Allow time to let each design choice settle into place.

> **Choose standard sizes and shapes in a consistent palette.** Standard sizes are usually the best buy. For example, stone and ceramic tiles in stock sizes are usually less expensive than large slabs or small mosaics. Using standard sizes in a neutral palette for furnishings can also give you future design flexibility when you remodel or move. An 8 x 10-foot area rug in a neutral color is likely to work well in a variety of applications.

OPPOSITE Crown molding refines this lovely room by concealing the drapery hardware. Floor-to-ceiling draperies maximize the sense of space by adding height and drawing the eye into the farthest corner. A faux-painted armoire from another room, vibrant color and pattern, lamps made from inexpensive milk-paint candlesticks, and a side table (an old chest covered with fabric) add even more charm.
Design: Sabrina Balsky Interior Design Inc.

ABOVE While this custom-designed vanity of polished metals, etched glass, and maple is the star of the show, less-expensive materials such as standard-size white ceramic field tiles and slate floor tiles play supporting roles beautifully. The matching maple window and mirror frames provide another beautiful yet economical finishing touch.
Design: Andre Rothblatt

RIGHT Bead-board wainscoting, a thin band of white molding just below the ceiling, and the perfect shade of green are economical counterpoints to the handsome silver-footed tub and European faucet in this vintage bathroom.
Design: Jim Ross

> **Learn from current trends (but don't necessarily follow them).** Only a select few of the best and brightest new trends will have long-term staying power. Classic choices bring lasting aesthetic and economic satisfaction. So as new ideas come along, be sure they fit into the context of your life and your overall design plans before you invest in them. Besides, if that hot new trend is really here to stay, you'll have plenty of time to determine whether it's right for you.

> **Avoid last-minute construction changes.** While catching mistakes and making little shifts at just the right moment during the construction process can save time, money, and aggravation, extreme changes of direction may break the bank.

ABOVE On the landing just outside the master suite, unused space becomes an attractive and functional window seat providing extra storage for out-of-season sweaters.
Design: Sally Weston

RIGHT Pine plywood and bold geometry join forces, maximizing a narrow footprint.
Design: Emilio Lopez and Monica Ribera

RIGHT Staying true to its origins, this design collected all its ideas from the past, then, without great expense, polished them for maximum storage and light. The cabinet on the left was purchased unfinished, painted by the homeowner, and detailed with reproduction hardware. The small stained-glass panel makes a beautiful design statement at a fraction of the cost of a full window.
Design: Leslie Markman-Stern

➤ **Make choices that work overtime.** A decorative chest at the foot of the bed is not only pretty to look at; it can also store small suitcases and give you a place to sit and tie your shoes. Plants at the window soften your decor, screen the natural light, and provide sheltering privacy. A cabinet for extra blankets that also houses a pop-up TV can serve as a room divider as well. Whenever one design element can perform a double function, the only thing for you to figure out is how it can perform a third!

> **Be discriminating: choose quality.** One of the best ways to save money is to buy things that will last. Intelligent spending often means choosing "fewer but finer." Pay close attention to details and craftsmanship and invest in products and materials that will endure.

> **Choose a style that suits your pocketbook.** Certain styles have built-in economies. A minimalist aesthetic can save you money if you really keep it minimal, and an eclectic or shabby chic approach allows you to scour flea markets and bargain-hunt. That vintage bedroom set you inherited from your grandmother may serve as the inspiration for the style of your new master suite or guest room.

> **Paint a new picture.** The most economical way to redecorate a room is with a fresh coat of paint. At less cost per square foot than anything else (other than soap and water), a new paint job renews and invigorates. And because of the power of color, every motion with the paintbrush puts emotion on the walls.

Final Thoughts

Whether you live in a cottage or a castle, reaching your design goals requires patience. Hold on to your vision, realizing it in phases if necessary, and selecting just one perfect piece at a time rather than assembling a roomful of compromises. Learn to savor the quiet promise of an empty corner.

Remember that spending less money on your bed and bath doesn't mean spending less creativity or enthusiasm. The search for economical and affordable solutions can often lead you to a wholly new and exciting design vision.

BELOW Making every corner count in a small space, a glazed cabinet adds storage and visual texture without compromising the sense of openness in the room.
Design: Sally Weston

OPPOSITE These unadorned windows bow to the beauty of nature, while also eliminating the extra expense of window coverings.
Design: Erica Broberg Architect

Design ideas are everywhere!

ABOVE A love of luxury and fine French perfume inspired this elegant bathroom vignette.
Design: Sandra Nunnerley Inc.

OPPOSITE The idea for this warehouse aesthetic came from . . . a warehouse, and from a strong desire to recycle urban leftovers ethically and artfully.
Design: LOT/EK

five

collecting ideas

really good ideas are often hard to find because they're hidden . . . in plain sight. The secret is learning to spot them! The pleasure — and the playfulness — of exploring the world in search of good design ideas can quickly become an unbreakable lifetime habit. As any idea collector will tell you, inspiration is everywhere, especially where you least expect to find it. Best of all, design isn't just something to look at — it's something to *do!*

Everything you see, feel, touch, smell, and taste has the potential to be transformed or adapted into your next bedroom or bath design statement. The pattern for your bathroom tile may repeat the rhythms and textures of your favorite winter scarf; a new bedroom color scheme can come from an old childhood memory; and the style you choose for your guest room might be sparked by brand-new materials or technologies.

Ideas can seem to spring from nowhere or can
come from very specific sources, such as a piece of art or furniture, a favorite collection, or the hardware you choose for your bathroom cabinetry. Ideas can come from exploring the world, your neighborhood, or your backyard. Surprising new concepts often result from collaboration, from the need to solve an unexpected design problem, or from restraints upon time or money. Ideas can come from your lifestyle, your goals for the future, a grand piece of music, or something as humble as a paper clip.

Ideas Come from Pictures

Most of us start collecting ideas by tearing pictures from magazines. Here are some ways to make that activity even more productive.

➢ Don't limit yourself to pictures of bedrooms and bathrooms. Give every image a chance. You may find the perfect decorative hardware for your bed or bath in a photograph of a kitchen.

➢ Save every image you love. Do you find yourself drawn to travel photos, images of nature, or pictures filled with people? You may not understand why something appeals to you now, but eventually patterns will emerge — patterns that hold important design clues.

➢ Save pictures you don't like! These can provide you and your design team with invaluable shortcuts to understanding your tastes.

➢ Don't reject a photograph until you've studied it carefully. You may not like the brash colors you first notice, but the clerestory windows may be just the architectural enhancement your bedroom needs. The floral wallpaper may be overwhelming, but the furniture arrangement around the fireplace might be just what you've been looking for. Train your eye. Challenge yourself to find at least one good idea in every picture. Then try the opposite: It's even more difficult to find design flaws in pictures you love!

LEFT AND OPPOSITE Borrowing inspiration from the mystery and beauty of the ruins left on the Colorado landscape by the Anasazi culture, the master bathroom shown on these pages is at once sheltering and open to the outdoors. Exterior walls of moss stone suddenly become interior walls in this delicate blend of ideas from nature and architecture.
Design: Alexander Gorlin Architects

Ideas Come from Architecture

Public buildings, architectural landmarks, churches, factories, homes — all are rich sources of ideas. The color scheme for my own bed and bath was inspired by a family trip to the Pazzi Chapel in Florence, Italy. I know of a master suite sitting room whose minimalist decor was copied from a small screening room in an art museum.

You can also take design cues from the interior and exterior architecture of your own home. Thoughtful repetition of its materials and motifs in your bedroom and bath can add beauty while gracefully integrating the design of these new rooms into your home.

LEFT AND BELOW The marine motif in this bathroom originated in the lush Art Deco designs of the 1920s. Stylized seaweed in pewter-plated steel decorates the tub and shower enclosure; plaster waves and bubbling water adorn the walls and crown molding; and shells are referenced in the sconces, the upholstery, and the scalloped mahogany vanity. Countertop openings for waste paper and refuse were inspired by airplane lavatories.
Design: Ronald Bricke

Ideas Come from Nature

Most beautiful design ideas have their roots in nature. There is no richer source of inspiration. Learning to track our responses to the world around us is a great way to find the colors, forms, textures, and patterns with which to create the rooms we want to live in.

Ideas Come from Travel Adventures

Some of the best souvenirs are the ideas we collect on our travels. Adventures at home and abroad can offer fresh new ways to look at life, architecture, and design, influencing the function of our rooms as well as their appearance. A Japanese soaking tub in your new bathroom is not only a beautiful design statement but can also affect your daily habits, and even your personal philosophy.

ABOVE The owners of this residence wanted to bring Tuscany home. The colonnade leading to the master suite is echoed in the vaulted bathroom.
Design: Nasrallah Fine Architectural Design

RIGHT Walls are faux-finished in a soft olive green, while beige stone floors and a carved mantel over the fireplace enhance the Mediterranean feel. Built into the cabinetry are sophisticated low-voltage lighting and an audio/video system. The style is old world, but the lifestyle it serves is definitely modern.
Design: Nasrallah Fine Architectural Design

LEFT Sitting next to a large and gracious foyer, a modestly scaled powder room is enlivened by color. Layering together ideas from separate rooms, the designer combined the vivid palette of two lithographs in the adjoining bedroom with the geometric grid from the existing gray tile to unify the aesthetic throughout this New York City apartment.
Design: Jamie Drake

Ideas Come from the People, Places, and Things You Love

Bed and bath design ideas can come from the texture of a basket, a needlepoint pillow, your favorite lithograph, the color of your eyes, or just about anything else!

OPPOSITE Inspired by the theatricality of a glamorous Paris nightspot, this room transports guests to another world. Warm copper, gold, and hot orange play against electric blue and silver. Silks and velvets are ornamented and tasseled. Hammered brass horses from India, Moroccan silver cones, an armoire made in China, a miniature elephant carrying a parasol, and diaphanous chiffon on silver poles with elaborate finials complete this exotic bedroom.
Design: Joe Lehman and Martha Hatrak

RIGHT Can you name one good design idea in this picture? This bathroom names two: Richard and Whitney. This design was also inspired by two more New York City names: Yellow and Checker.
Design: Joan Halperin/Interior Design

LEFT This bed, inspired by a 1940s wood-paneled station wagon, is detailed down to the metal grommets that accent its two-tone frame. Complemented by art, textiles, and classic bentwood pieces, the massive bed is the centerpiece of the room. The free-form mosaic pattern of the fireplace surround, which repeats the earthy palette of gold, copper, crimson, blue, and green, was the spontaneous creation of the designer.
Design: Linda C. Golden

RIGHT New ideas can be just under your nose — so close you can smell them. Wishing to set this vacation spa apart from other retreats, the design team turned to its historic gardens for inspiration. The charming flowerpot sinks, with art and accessories to match, make the new locker room feel like an old-fashioned potting shed. In the next room, guests refresh themselves under whimsical sunflower-shaped showerheads.
Design: Ray Snyder Designs

LEFT In this Moroccan-inspired show house bedroom, a sumptuous four-poster bed is strewn with sensual satins and silks in a dramatic palette of deep ambers and indigos.
Design: Clodagh

BELOW The oblique arc of this bathroom alcove ceiling echoes the curves of the medicine cabinet and the white porcelain pedestal sink below. The cabinets to the left were constructed of the same wood used in the mirror frame, and each drawer was sized separately to fit the specific needs of the homeowner's wardrobe.
Design: William and Colette Rodon Hornof

Show Houses Are a Rich Source of Ideas

When designers are given free rein, their visions can be intoxicating. Show houses allow designers to explore ideas and express their creativity in unexpected new ways.

OPPOSITE Rather than fret over the massive girder in the master bedroom or hide it with cabinetry (which would impinge on the open space), the choice was made to relish the beauty of its functional power. The sharp contrast between the architectural truth of the raw space and the softer elements of this design is one of the room's visual strengths.
Design: Asfour Guzy Architects

New Ideas Come from Solving Problems

The energy that is stirred up as problems arise can be a great source of new solutions, the pressure of frustration often leading to inspiration.

ABOVE When a designer wants to make a splash, ideas can spill over onto the floor!
Design: Wendy Gardner and Stephen Gardner

RIGHT The design challenges: intense red walls and an orange-toned floor that "had to stay," insufficient space for the bed frame, and architecture that was not plumb and level. The solutions: white carpet over the floor, red-and-white toile to soften the red wall color as it moves to the bed and love seat, and window treatments to hide the short wall behind the bed and camouflage discrepancies in window frame heights.
Design: Karen Padgett Prewitt

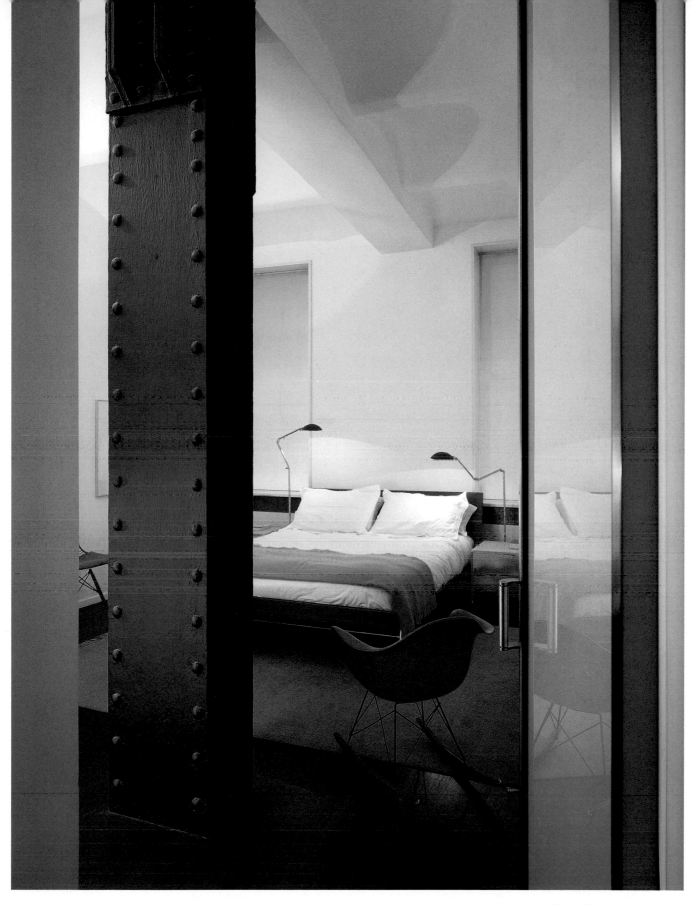

Ideas can come from rooms you visit. Here are ten good ideas drawn from this master suite. See what else you can find!

➤ A neutral color palette allows for a wide and flexible combination of textured and patterned materials.

➤ Wall-mounted lamps at the bedside work with or without side tables.

➤ Contrasting pieces, such as a desk at one side of the bed and a covered table on the other, add variety.

➤ Unexpected design elements — the faux leopard and zebra prints — can impart a touch of drama.

➤ Fireplaces always anchor the design of a room, contributing presence and a sense of permanence.

➤ Crown molding and ceiling planes can be used to define separate spaces within a room.

➤ The ten-light French door provides privacy for the water closet while still admitting light.

> Bathrooms can be furnished like any other room. These rich, walnut-stained oak floors and the cozy reading area would be equally at home in a bedroom, library, living room, or den.

> Designing the bathroom vanity to look like a piece of fine furniture (even down to refinements such as the crystal pulls on the vanity drawers) can make it a focal point of your room.

> Architectural niches with glass shelves add depth and elegance to this bathroom.

OPPOSITE, ABOVE, AND LEFT
Caution: Because it will stimulate your curiosity and delight your imagination, the search for new architectural and design ideas may become habit-forming.
Design: Stuart Cohen & Julie Hacker Architects and Stephanie Wohlner Design

ABOVE This loft space is defined by its freestanding interior elements. Homeowner and video artist Frank Snider gave free rein to his own creative impulses by designing and hand-stitching the rich cashmere bedspread from $6 sweaters he bought at a Salvation Army store. This spread of "pure luxury" measures 4 by 6 sweaters (plus one dress).
Design: Resolution: 4 Architecture

OPPOSITE Handsome primitive masks collected over twenty-five years of travels inspired architectural as well as decorative decisions in this master suite.
Design: Olson Sundberg Kundig Allen Architects and Ted Tuttle Interior Design

Ideas Can Grow Over Time

Collections of art, antiques, family mementos, photos — anything that is sought after and saved can inspire good design ideas.

Final Thoughts

The best thing about collecting ideas is that you'll never have to pay for them, dust them, or find a place to display them until you decide they're absolutely right for you. Besides, having a good idea and then letting it go can be as exhilarating — and far more liberating — than possessing it.

Choosing your style is like dancing the hokey-pokey – you put your whole self in!

ABOVE With a clean view of the Manhattan skyline, this shower design is stripped down to the bare essentials.
Design: Mojo Stumer Associates

OPPOSITE Fabricated using shipbuilding techniques, this sunken tub bathes its owner in the natural warmth of honey-colored teak.
Design: Woodmeister Corporation

except for your terry cloth bath towel and your night-clothes, nothing in your home comes closer to your skin than the rooms that bathe and embrace you. Our bodies know the smooth comfort of cotton, the gentle give of down, the reassuring heft of wool. We remember the satiny borders of blankets pulled all the way up to our noses, the delicate texture of embroidered linens, and the loopy afghans knit by our grandmothers. We respond differently to wicker chairs than to chintz cushions or an ottoman made of leather. Shiny metals, polished stones, woods of all kinds — each has a feel all its own.

So let's take a tour of some bathtubs, showers, and beds. Trying each one on for size, it's time your palms, elbows, shoulders, fingertips, back, and even your little toe have their say.

six

choosing your style

LEFT Variegated blue, green, and gold slate tiles dominate the design of this earthy grottolike master bathroom. With just enough space for the large tub-for-two, the choice was made to mirror the flanking walls to create the illusion of more slate as well as a more open sense of space and light.
Design: Ausberg Interiors

RIGHT Personalized with robin's-egg blue and just a touch of gold leaf, this antique four-poster bed with an unadorned canopy frame basks in the golden glow from a mica shade on the earthenware lamp. Hickory pecan floorboards and pine furniture continue the natural simplicity of this design.
Design: Michelle Pheasant Design, Inc.

RIGHT Adding stylish theatricality and glamour, this freestanding shower silo, with open door and an elevated showerhead, creates a feeling of weighty protection with its thick, curved Carrara marble wall. Lined with the same hexagonal tiles that cover the floor, and accented with bands of contrasting 2-inch square tiles, it represents a bold departure from traditional bathroom floor plans.
Design: Laura Bohn Design Associates

LEFT Recessed into an illuminated niche, and flanked by side tables and reading lamps, this upholstered bed with a winged headboard has a glorious view of the garden through two window walls that meet in the corner. The handsome metal fireplace (with an exterior chimney) and beamed wooden ceiling enhance the cozy warmth of this small space.
Design: The Wiseman Group and Scott Williams

LEFT Complemented by the sparkle of a classic English faucet on the tub, blue-and-white vessel sinks patterned like fine china, silver accessories, and wall-mounted vanity fixtures that might have been found in a country farmhouse, this design has multiple layers of white on white: bead board, marble, solid surfacing, and porcelain.
Design: Leslie S. Saul

RIGHT Sitting on a floor of tumbled marble, and surrounded by walls of roughly textured brick without mortar, this elliptical tub is the essence of smooth and seamless comfort. Separate shower and water closets are enclosed behind custom metal and etched-glass doors, with warm red-toned wood framing the window and a wisp of willow tucked in the corner.
Design: John Petrarca

LEFT Between pillars with illuminated niches that serve as side tables, this bed divides the space between the sleeping/sitting area and the home office behind it. In addition to a three-bridge view of San Francisco Bay, there is a second view overhead, of the extraordinary tongue-and-groove redwood pyramid ceiling.
Design: Kendall Wilkinson Design

RIGHT With the look of a fine European antique, the stepped design of this custom vanity is echoed in the medicine cabinet above with its three mirrored doors. Finished with delicately veined marble, raised-panel inset doors, and brass hardware, it brings grand style to a modestly scaled New York City master bathroom.
Design: Cullman and Kravis, Inc., and John B. Murray Architects

RIGHT This custom stainless steel soaking tub combines high-tech materiality with the grace of its Japanese-inspired aesthetic. Set into a black granite ledge, it opens to the bedroom on one side and the living room with its skyscraper views on the other. Illuminated by recessed cove lighting, the tub can be enclosed for privacy by sliding shoji-screen pocket doors.
Design: Brininstool + Lynch

BELOW All the elements of this design, including the concrete ceiling and the concrete-bordered bamboo floor, bow in humility to the beauty of nature. Using fixed louvers and windows sheathed in protective film, engineering and aesthetics team up to control the heat from the Florida sun in this guesthouse overlooking Little Sarasota Bay.
Design: Toshiko Mori Architect

LEFT In a cozy corner of an upstairs bedroom, an imposing headboard with inset panel, elaborate moldings, hand-carved finials, and an arched crown, along with a matching wooden side table, offers guests an inviting blend of downy comfort and Victorian formality.
Design: Erica Broberg Architect and Ruth Ann McSpadden

ABOVE With a feeling of casual country styling created by the leafy Arts and Crafts wall covering, natural materials, bead board, and a touch of ivy, this bathroom owes its architectural strength to the well-articulated forms of the deep-set window, the built-in tub surround, and the slotted step with scalloped feet.
Design: Laura Bohn Design Associates

LEFT This bathroom design owes its strength and beauty to the careful attention that was paid to each architectural detail. The tub, in an alcove formed by the glass-walled shower and the water closet, is backed with wainscoting, enclosed with double-recessed panels, and topped with Carrara marble. Crown molding and an oval clerestory window further refine the space.
Design: Jan Gleysteen Architects, Inc.

RIGHT With an equal measure of crisp color and classic form, this diminutive guest room is bathed in sunshine even on cloudy days. The joyful chrome-yellow bed, bedding, and walls, with an accent of red in the blanket, are juxtaposed to the rigorous simplicity of the early-twentieth-century Mackintosh Hill House chair and Rietveld crate table.
Design: Stamberg Aferiat Architecture

BELOW Strong, clean lines and rich materials combine to create this handsome contemporary design. There is abundant energy in the flamelike veining of the highly polished earth-toned marble, providing a strong contrast with the limestone floor and white fixtures. An alcove for the tub, with its classic English faucet, is elegantly defined by two panels of etched and clear glass.
Design: Scott Himmel, Architect P.C.

RIGHT Enclosed in a warm yellow and cool green garden of softly gathered florals, this sheltering canopy bed is the centerpiece of a master bedroom suite that was designed as a quiet personal retreat. Matching fabric was used for the window treatment, and all the accessories were carefully chosen to maintain an ambience of serene harmony.
Design: Robinson & Shades Design Group

RIGHT A round window with spoked mullions, a glass display cabinet, a scalloped vanity table with glass legs, and a crystal chandelier suspended from a dome detailed with a necklace of mirrored tiles impart a stately elegance to this bathroom. The gray terry cloth chair adds comfort, and a steam shower provides a distinctly modern amenity.
Design: Fox-Nahem Design

LEFT Screened by the treetops, this second-story bathroom, with its striking claw-foot tub and integrated shower, was designed with a sense of nineteenth-century romance. Light is amplified by a mirrored wall that surrounds the window and by the metallic tub finish, and chrome fixtures are complemented by natural stones of rust and beige.
Design: Eddie Saunders

Final Thoughts

In a word, choosing your style is . . . *sensational*. Use all your senses to ensure that the look, feel, sound, and scent of your new design is just right. When your body agrees with your mind, you know that you've found *your* style.

LEFT A white oval tub floats on a wavy sea of blue ceramic tiles. This vivacious design brings energy and light to a windowless interior space. The shower is built into a cavelike recess at the foot of the tub, so that no door is required.
Design: Alexander Gorlin Architects

ABOVE With its Romeo and Juliet balcony and a narrow skylight that splays open to admit more natural light during the day and a view of the stars at night, this tiny attic bedroom, finished in white with undertones of wheat, sets a gently romantic tone. The ceiling begins its pitch just 5 feet from the floor, then soars dramatically.
Design: Andre Rothblatt

The shared excitement of the creative process turns teamwork into team play, and problem solving into fun!

ABOVE With poetic precision, this closet has a place for everything. Expert detailing continues on walls defined by 1/4-inch reveals above 8-inch flush baseboards.

OPPOSITE When the shoji-screen doors are open, this bedroom is flooded with natural light and enjoys a wonderful city view. Design: Peter Sollogub and Maho Abe (all images in chapter)

While successful designs vary widely, successful design teams often look and feel very much the same. Inevitably, there is a quiet understanding and mutual respect among the homeowner and each artist, craftsperson, consultant, and strategist that permits all of them to thrive. And the common thread is that everyone listens to everyone else.

Design help is widely available today. In addition to asking for references from friends and family, you can find many manufacturers and retailers who offer professional assistance. Organizations such as the National Kitchen & Bath Association, the American Institute of Architects, and the American Society of Interior Designers can also help you put the right design team together.

This chapter begins with the story of a truly successful design collaboration, and also includes tips for choosing your design team and surviving construction.

seven

your design team

LEFT The hardware for the woven curtain in the bay of the study is concealed in the recess surrounding the floating ceiling plane.

RIGHT To separate the bedroom from the study and still maintain a sense of openness, a structural column was hidden in cabinetry that also incorporates storage and a desk. A sliding shoji-screen partition, made of rhya rosa wood and milk-white glass, provides privacy for the bedroom.

It occurred to me today that although design is a real-world process that always involves a measure of serious struggle, when it's over most good design teams seem to remember only the joy of it all. That certainly was the case with film producer Mitchell Robbins's fabulous Boston apartment.

Despite the fact that the building was under construction and he had been alerted to its complicated structural issues, Mitchell knew that he had found the perfect space for his new apartment. Loving Boston as he does, he had to have the incredible view of Copley Square that the space offered. The dynamic energy of this unique panorama was sure to nurture his creative spirit, and he had a clear idea of how he wanted the interior spaces to work. Mitchell had expected to buy a larger apartment, but for a bachelor who uses his home primarily as a retreat in which to study and write, this place was too good to pass up.

Mitchell began by doing his homework. Knowing that he wanted to transform a standard three-bedroom unit into a loftlike space, he pored through magazines, tearing out every image he liked. "I think it's important to provide that type of communication to your team. Otherwise you're just throwing out words, such as 'I want it to be open,' or 'I want it to be light.' I think you should be able to describe those words in a picture form."

At their very first meeting, Mitchell was not only able to show his team the look he was after, but he went one giant step further. Taking a break from their conversation, he asked the whole team — including principal-in-charge Peter Sollogub and Gretchen McPhee, an architect at his firm; interior designer Maho Abe and her associate Rina Okawa; client representative Lorraine Sweeney; general contractor Geir Boger; and project manager Ginette Castro — to listen, not to him, but to his favorite CD. That was the breakthrough moment that everyone still remembers . . . the moment the design began to crystallize.

> "It was really important that I work with a team that could conceptualize what I was feeling," says Mitchell. "I said, 'Peter, I want you to forget about all of the other things you've been working on, I want you to just listen to the music and *think* what I'm *feeling*. I want to feel this type of vibe when I'm in my place.'"

As Peter recalls this moment, "He had chosen a Latin piece, soft and bright, a flowing, lyrical composition entwined with musical ebbs and pockets of melodies. As we listened, he said, 'That's what I want.' It was this moment that provided the foundation for the entire design strategy."

Inspired by the music and using movable walls and carefully articulated ceiling heights, Peter configured the apartment with an open plan that allows one space to flow freely into another while highlighting the city views. Having movable boundaries between public and private areas allows his client to comfortably use all the space himself when he's working (his favorite spot is actually in the corner of the living room couch, where he can read, write, or review tapes on the flat-screen TV). And for entertaining guests, the circulation patterns and the fantastic city views are equally wonderful.

Interior designer Maho Abe's minimalist instincts and perfectionist's eye for detail played perfectly into these spaces and into Mitchell's desire for harmony. This is a clean, uncluttered look with a serene arrangement of colors and materials. Maho prefers a pared-down look herself, but laughingly admits, "I don't like edges — lines, lines, lines. So I use color and material to create comfort and elegance." Her softening palette included maple and a pearly onyx in the bathroom, ribbon-striped mahogany and rhya rosa wood in the dressing room, and mahogany and textured paint in the bedroom (with traditional Japanese red lacquer finishes inside the cabinets in the study). The French limestone floor and baseboards in the bathroom blend perfectly with the neutral carpeting Maho used throughout the rest of the suite.

Wonderfully pleased with the results that he and his team achieved, Mitchell attributes much of that success to regular meetings in which they "reviewed, and reviewed, and reviewed" each stage of the project. And as Maho observes, "The client is a film producer, and he treated this architectural project the same way he makes his movies. He acted like a producer, using us as the team to create his dream. He respected everybody's opinions, and was very open and receptive to new ideas."

"What I'm most proud about," says Mitchell, "is that we actually ended up getting the feeling I was after. This is where I come to get away from the intensity of my office so that I am able to write in a more contemplative environment, and the space serves one hundred percent in the way I wanted it to serve."

Joan's Five Rules of Thumb

These few simple rules will prepare you for design success on any project large or small, whether you're remodeling, renovating, or building anew.

❶ Assume Nothing

Making assumptions is like trying to find a shortcut through dense woods; it's tempting, but you run the risk of getting lost. For example, just because your friend is thrilled with the work of a particular interior decorator, don't assume that you will work well with that person. Think long and hard before you choose members for your design team. Are their personalities compatible with yours? Will they understand your point of view and respect your needs and opinions? Do you like the work they've done for their other clients?

This rule applies to every step in the design and construction process. Don't assume that the beautiful faucet or duvet cover you've always wanted is still being made, or that your contractor will consider daily cleanup to be part of his job. It's wise to take nothing for granted.

❷ Never Take No for an Answer (at Least Not Right Away)

When someone says, "It can't be done," remember that design problems often have unexpected solutions. Before you accept no for an answer, take extra time to think things through; there may be a yes out there. Talk to others, or try to come up with a solution of your own. Precisely because you're not a professional, you may discover an unconventional solution.

As one home improvement enthusiast I know wisely observes, "No one cares more about your home than you." A self-reliant frame of mind is invaluable in designing bedrooms and bathrooms that satisfy your expectations. Bring your own focused intelligence and creativity to bear on the problem. You'll be amazed at what you come up with!

❸ Never Take Yes for an Answer Either

Even small-scale projects can become extremely complex, pulling your attention in several different directions at once. When this happens, it's tempting to take yes for an answer without making absolutely sure that your instructions and wishes are clearly understood. It is easy to accept assurances that everything is going along according to your specifications and schedule without checking for yourself. But be watchful! Reviewing the work in progress, asking questions, and clarifying instructions will save you time, money, and regret.

❹ Be Unsophisticated

There is no such thing as a dumb question when it comes to getting the new bedroom and bath you want. Your expertise will grow over time, so don't be embarrassed to ask questions. This is especially true when dealing with buzzwords. If a designer or contractor uses words or concepts you don't understand, stop the conversation and ask for an explanation. Avoid the temptation to nod your head and smile knowingly when you don't fully comprehend something. You owe it to yourself — and your pocketbook — to be unsophisticated.

❺ Think Backward

It's easy to look ahead when you start a design project, imagining that glorious day when you will walk into your wonderful new bathroom and fill the tub with bubbles. But when it comes to the rough-and-tumble construction phase, you'll be in much better shape if you also remember to think backward in the planning stage.

Once you have envisioned your final design goal, work backward to break it down into all of the many tasks that must be accomplished in order to achieve that goal. Something as simple as a new wall-mounted light fixture for your bedroom requires sourcing, ordering, delivery, and installation, and may also require new wiring, plastering, and painting.

Even if your designer and contractor will be taking responsibility for most of this work, thinking backward and identifying all the steps involved in your project *before* you get started can help you be a more effective leader of your design team, and give you a big boost in getting the job done on time, on budget, and to your satisfaction.

More Tips

Here are more tips on choosing and working with your design team and on surviving construction.

Your Design Team

➤ Every design project takes teamwork. Even stouthearted, self-reliant "I-can-do-this-all-by-myselfers" seek counsel and support from time to time. And help is everywhere! In today's competitive marketplace, many retailers and manufacturers often offer free design advice on-site, on the web, and by phone.

➤ When asking for personal recommendations for team members, ask for three at a time. Someone else's second choice may be solid gold to you. Ask your friends if they were "unconditionally satisfied" with the people they worked with, and if the fees they paid matched the results. Base your decisions on detailed information, and pay particular attention to rave reviews.

➤ Choose people who are as highly trained as possible. If the scope of your project justifies it, specialists such as lighting designers or faux-finishers can help you avoid costly mistakes. And getting things right the first time saves money.

➤ Ask for multiple references for each prospective member of your design team, and to see photographs of their work. Visiting their completed projects can be invaluable, and dropping in on them while they're working on a project can tell you volumes as to how they run a job.

➤ Every project has its share of unexpected problems — even a "dream job" can have a little nightmare or two. Ask interviewees for examples of how they've solved problems in the past. You can learn a lot from their answers (as well as from their willingness to share these revealing stories).

➤ You must feel a personal connection with your designer, and have a strong sense that the listening will go both ways. Remember that a good designer challenges clients to stretch their tastes, but good clients challenge designers as well. Follow the same instincts you would on a first date. If the chemistry is wrong, move on with no regrets.

Surviving Construction

➤ Be realistic and try to keep smiling. Think of the construction process as "creative chaos." Remember that every problem has a solution. You may be pleasantly surprised to discover that "mistakes" can often lead to unforeseen and innovative results.

➤ Decide in advance on the chain of command — what role you and every other member of the team will play during the weeks or months ahead, and how decisions will be made. Clear systems for allocating responsibilities, communicating, and making payments will protect against unnecessary conflicts or surprises. Signed change orders are particularly helpful in tracking costs.

➤ Once construction begins, trust yourself and your team, allowing everyone the freedom to work in his or her own way.

➤ Try to remain flexible and open to new ideas suggested by your team members as work proceeds. But remember that major changes once you're under way can cause serious budgetary overruns. Take all the time you need in advance to detail every aspect of your design plan.

➤ Be diligent about visiting the construction site. And when you catch a mistake, resist the temptation to "live with it" — at least until you've examined all your options. Even a major mistake, when spotted early enough, can be relatively

RIGHT With a convertible couch and its own bathroom, the guest bedroom is as multifunctional as every other space in this home. Directly accessible from the bar, dining area, kitchen, living room, and master suite (with sliding, shoji-screen "movable walls" for privacy), this room continues the uninterrupted circulation throughout the apartment.

LEFT The extraordinary vanity of luminous onyx is the centerpiece of this master bathroom. The custom gridwork on the cabinets is repeated in several rooms throughout the apartment.

simple to fix. For example, when you notice that a window has been framed too high, reframing it can be relatively easy, while "letting it go" can seriously affect the view forever.

➤ Have regularly scheduled face-to-face meetings with your team to discuss goals, budgeting concerns, and scheduling issues. I know some homeowners who attribute the success of their remodeling project to *daily* meetings with their contractor.

➤ If possible, don't move out of your house during a remodeling. Being there each day will not only help you spot issues as they arise, but can also have a positive impact on your team's morale.

➤ Allow ample time to clear out your bedrooms and bathrooms prior to construction. Don't do it the night before your builder is scheduled to arrive! Pack and label everything with time to spare, taking stock of your wardrobe, toiletries, books, and other personal items, and reorganizing them for proper placement in your new rooms. You may find that the necessities you *don't* pack away are all you really want to keep.

➤ Because delays are an inevitable part of the building process, try not to let the demolition work begin until all your raw materials, new cabinets, and fixtures are ready for delivery.

➤ Prepare for construction by providing the crew with a dedicated entryway, restroom, and convenient space for snacks and lunch.

➤ Make sure your construction area is sealed off with at least two layers of plastic sheeting, with damp towels at the bottom, to control dust. Floor mats for wiping shoes are helpful both inside and outside the work area, and removing pictures from walls in adjacent rooms is a good way to prevent accidental damage.

➤ Clarify in advance the procedures for daily site cleanup and safety.

➤ Minimize the disruption to your personal and family life by maintaining your daily routines. Although your commitment to your bed and bath project may be boundless, other family members may have less vision and patience.

➤ When the pressure builds, find a way to regenerate. Regain your perspective by spending a night in a charming bed-and-breakfast, taking an architectural tour, or splurging on some inspiring new design magazines and books that will rekindle your enthusiasm.

➤ Don't invite houseguests for the day after your scheduled completion date.

➤ And most important of all, remember that in the realm of all possible problems, design problems are good problems to have.

Final Thoughts

One of the most enthralling aspects of interviewing homeowners, architects, and designers for my TV shows and books is hearing their exciting stories about the creative process itself. While we've all heard the occasional design horror story, what I hear most often are extraordinary tales of the joys of collaboration. When the team is right, each individual contributes his or her unique talents and perspective toward a common goal. The result is not only a beautiful room, but wonderful shared memories as well.

part two:

the five building blocks of bed & bath design

Let beauty follow function into your bedrooms and baths.

t he first and most fundamental question in bed and bath design is, "How will these rooms be used?" While every bedroom is for sleeping and every bathroom is for bathing, today's lifestyles call for rooms with more functional diversity than ever. If space is limited, we're asking rooms to multitask just as we do. In larger homes, we're building suites that serve as private apartments, catering to the complex demands of the day, then graciously caring for us when day is done.

As you plan these personal rooms, ask yourself how you want to spend your hours in them. Exercise areas, work spaces, entertainment centers, sitting areas, satellite kitchens, saunas, and steam showers are just some of ways in which their functionality can be expanded. As you balance questions of practicality and aesthetics, consider the true beauty of convenience and comfort.

ABOVE The architectural refinements in this fully equipped gym in an eight-room master suite make any workout more pleasant.
Design: Cullman and Kravis, Inc., and Rosenblum Architects

OPPOSITE This homeowner bathes in the beauty of natural light.
Design: Stuart Cohen & Julie Hacker Architects

eight

function

Functionality in the bath and closet area is separated into three zones: a shower/tub/toilet area; a grooming area with a sink and shallow drawers for socks, underwear, and miscellaneous accessories; and an area for hanging clothes and storing shoes. Bruce says that using space intelligently can give you much more storage than you ever thought possible. "People often move because they think they need more space, so I like to give them more space than they can possibly use. That avoids the hassle of moving."

Designer Bruce Bierman believes in putting function first. According to Bruce, if you want to know how your designer thinks, you should see how he designs for himself. That's why he often invites new clients to tour his loft in New York's Flatiron District. "I designed my loft for my lifestyle, not for entertaining," he says. "Too many people design only for occasion-driven events; I design for real life."

The first response most people have to his highly functional, well-ordered apartment is always the same: "I feel like I'm on a yacht." For Bruce, the more that form follows function, the better! To get the form just right requires a laserlike attention to detail. In his dressing area, for example, Bruce took an inventory of every object he uses and every move he makes during his daily routine, then engineered spaces that have what he refers to as "intuitive logic" — a sense of order that makes it obvious where everything belongs.

OPPOSITE, RIGHT, AND BELOW
Tucked into a narrow corner, an
entertainment tower lets the
natural light bounce off a full-length
mirror framed in gold leaf, creating
the effect of a second window.
Next to the bed, a control panel
with intercom and phone operates
the electronics in the entire
apartment. The closet maximizes
utility with divided drawers and
glass shelves that make everything
easy to see and reach, while the
bathroom is designed to take
advantage of a vivacious city view.
Design: Bruce Bierman Design, Inc.

Work Areas

Do you occasionally work at home? If so, what are your work surface, filing, and storage requirements? If all you need is your briefcase and a laptop computer to keep up with deadlines, then you may find that a small writing desk in a corner, under a stairwell, or on the landing outside your room is adequate.

If you regularly work at home, there are many ways to equip your master bedroom with a work area without sacrificing style. Build a compact office into a closet, an armoire, or a custom cabinet. Cabinetry with a desk on one side can serve as a headboard on the other, efficiently separating zones in a small space. A sleeping loft above your desk or a Murphy bed are other ways to give yourself more work space in your bedroom.

RIGHT AND ABOVE A personal sitting room — the perfect place for quiet hours alone or afternoon tea with a friend — is also a home business center. The daybed adds extra versatility (convenient for napping children), and a few steps away a second, smaller staff office with coordinated furniture further increases function.
Design: Cullman and Kravis, Inc., and Rosenblum Architects

BELOW AND RIGHT In a walk-in closet, an inlaid French 1870s dressing table tiptoeing over a pastel Samarkand rug becomes a work surface when panels behind it open to reveal a high-tech home office. Cabinetry of French-polished primavera wood is offset by a ceiling of laminated glass and rice paper suspended from stainless steel beams.
Design: M (Group)

Entertainment Centers

The design principles that apply to work areas can also be used for entertainment centers. Technology can be integrated with any decor. TVs and stereos can pop up electronically from consoles at the foot of the bed, be recessed over the fireplace, or angled into a corner. Disguised as works of art, flat-screen TVs can hang on almost any wall.

Bathrooms are becoming as high-tech as the rest of the home. Stereos and telephones can be concealed in walls, cabinets, or drawers. TVs can even hide behind two-way mirrors over the vanity, appearing and disappearing with the flip of a switch.

ABOVE An easy chair, ottoman, and shelves of books waiting to be explored are all that's needed in this mezzanine sitting area overlooking Lake Erie.
Design: Emanuela Frattini Magnusson

Sitting Areas

Another lovely luxury in or near the bedroom is a separate seating area. Within these private confines, a chair or two, or perhaps a love seat or chaise, may be all that's needed to layer more function — as well as style — into your design.

RIGHT This restful bedroom, in airy white and neutral wood tones anchored with a touch of black, functions as a place for stillness. A long shelf solves the problem of where to place the bed in a room with large windows and narrow wall space.
Design: Clodagh

BELOW The initial inspiration for this decor came from the bright red linen storage boxes that now hold evening shoes and accessories. The diamond overlay on the side of the island repeats a motif used on glass transoms throughout the house.
Design: Jean Verbridge and Thaddeus Siemasko

Closets and Storage

Planning for adequate storage is a central issue in bed and bath design. Walk-in closets and dressing rooms are popular because of the wide range of storage solutions they offer. Built into one corner of a large suite, the ample dressing area shown at right enjoys natural light from three large windows. In the evening, two chandeliers imported from Italy illuminate the room. With the flexibility of adjustable bars for hanging, clothes can easily be rearranged. Shoes are discreetly tucked into cubbyholes on the hidden side of the small island, and just out of view, enclosed in matching mahogany cabinetry, is a small kitchen with coffeemaker, sink, two refrigerator drawers, and a compact dishwasher. There's also a fully equipped laundry room on the other side of the adjoining bathroom.

When space is at a premium, platform beds with built-in drawers and beds that hinge open to reveal spacious wells offer additional storage options. Storage can also be incorporated into headboards, footboards, benches, ottomans, or side tables.

Function meets elegance in the bedroom shown opposite, where a state-of-the-art media center, drawers for out-of-season storage and family albums, and even a built-in ironing board are concealed behind cabinet doors with a buttery glazed finish.

ABOVE A towel warmer dutifully stands guard between the dressing area and shower.
Design: Adolfo Perez, Architect

LEFT Based on a precise examination of the homeowner's requirements, custom cabinetry in this walk-through dressing room was tailored for a perfect fit.
Design: Donna Livingston Design

OPPOSITE Inspired by the paneled walls of the French boudoir style, these paneled built-ins open to reveal ample storage. The canopy ceiling, accented by decorative molding, creates a tentlike feeling. Window seats framed by arches and pilasters complete the intimate sense of enclosure.
Design: Jan Gleysteen Architects, Inc.

Whatever the size of your closet, organization is key. Arrange everything for convenient access; clothes can be organized by season, size, or color. Attractive storage can disguise clutter. Glass shelves and shallow drawers allow good visibility, so that items are easy to find. Do what you can to eliminate deep piles or densely packed rows of objects; out of sight usually means out of use.

Account for everything. Make room for all your linens, clothes, accessories, shoes, and boots. Be certain that your night table will accommodate your every need. If you've always wanted a water decanter next to the bed, give it a spot. In the bathroom, know where and how you plan to hang wet towels. Do you have a convenient place for a clothes hamper? Where will you collect items for dry cleaning?

For frequent travelers, life can be made less stressful with closet spaces that facilitate packing. Portable clothes racks and retractable hooks are valuable aids. Not having to search for suitcases, travel irons, steamers, and cosmetic cases also speeds up the process of getting ready for a trip.

RIGHT A pool house bath design makes subtle references to water with its gentle wooden waves on the walls and countertop and a splash of blue inside the vessel sink.
Design: Jean Verbridge and Thaddeus Siemasko

BELOW Covering the radiator under the bathroom window, a slotted bench warms both the room and the towels during winter months.
Design: Joan Halperin/Interior Design

Sharing Spaces

If you share your bedroom and bath, design for each person's needs. Finding ways to segregate sleeping spaces from dressing and grooming areas will lead to beautiful designs and beautiful relationships, especially if your schedules vary.

The cherrywood and pale-blond marble bath/dressing room shown at left was designed to give an early-rising husband the freedom to prepare for his day without disturbing his wife. The bureau was custom-built with easy-to-organize 6-inch-deep drawers, and the mirrored wall above it opens for more storage. A telephone, radio, and telescoping garment hook are built into the narrow wall between the dressing and bath areas. Recessed medicine cabinets flank the mirror above the vanity, which also provides additional storage. The curved-glass shower rounds out this functional design with six body sprays, shampoo niches, and a grab bar.

Guest Rooms

Do you have a large family, lots of overnight guests, or a household full of pets? If so, everybody needs a nest.

As children transition away from home, consider the rooms they leave behind. They can be converted to guest rooms, but if your own bedroom is right next door, the chance to create a bedroom suite by converting a vacated room to a media room, sitting area, library, or gym may be hard to pass up. I've heard young adults complain that their old bedroom became a walk-in closet within hours after they moved away!

Light and Sound

Bedrooms and baths need good general light, excellent task light for grooming and reading, and as much accent light as your decor requires. Also important is eliminating light when you don't want it. Blackout shades, lined curtains, venetian blinds, and electrically powered blinds that retract into soffits are excellent ways to block out the sun. Light switches at each entrance in both the bedroom and bathroom, and even next to the bed, are practical and convenient.

Because sound can also be an unwelcome intrusion, carefully consider where to place your bed. Be alert to ambient noise from other rooms or from outdoors.

Strategically concealing outlets inside drawers and cabinets can be an elegant way to let you store illuminated mirrors, hair dryers, and other appliances out of sight. Stylish surfaces that camouflage function make life easier and more beautiful. As much as you may need the many tools of modern life, tucking them out of sight can have a calming effect.

Maintenance

Ease of maintenance is an important functional consideration, so remember that elaborate layering of linens, spreads, and pillows that must be painstakingly tucked, folded, or otherwise arranged may not suit your daily schedule. A simple duvet may fit better with your lifestyle.

Integrated tissue dispensers and slots in the vanity top for an under-the-counter waste container are an attractive way to keep order. And be sure to check out the maintenance pros and cons of every material you choose — especially for the humid environment of the bathroom.

LEFT To accommodate elaborate rain forest showers that luxuriously deluge us from every angle, we are building bigger shower rooms, often for two.
Design: Jan Gleysteen Architects, Inc.

RIGHT As bathroom architecture has become more sophisticated, our bathrooms are even making their way into the great outdoors.

BELOW A steam shower unobtrusively introduces high function into this classic bathroom. The glass transom tilts open to allow steam to escape.
Design: Erica Broberg Architect

Rejuvenation and Healing

Good bed and bath designs — responsive to all our needs — not only inspire and support us at our best; they also nurture and protect us when we are tired or ill. By being sensitive to the psychological power of color, texture, forms, sounds, and scents, we can create beautiful, healing spaces. Sophisticated new technology allows us to build rooms that help care for our every need, so that we can soak, soothe, massage, cleanse, and rejuvenate in the comfort and privacy of our own homes.

LEFT Providing wheelchair
access does not mean giving
up any measure of style, and
today "universal" means
comfort for everybody.
Design: Chelly Bloom and Miguel A. Cruz

OPPOSITE Sometimes a breath of
fresh air is function enough.
Design: Andy Newman Architect

Universal Design

At one time, the term "universal design" referred only to
design that accommodated disabilities. But we are learning
that conveniences initially created to meet individual physical
challenges can help us all. By reexamining how we engineer
our bedrooms and bathrooms, we are also finding new paths to
beauty and convenience. Wider entryways and thresholds that
are flush to the floor, grab bars that are elegantly integrated
into bathroom designs, and toilets with advanced technology
and style are as aesthetically pleasing as they are practical, and
work well for everyone. Wishing to stay in our own homes as
long as possible as we age, we are beginning to build rooms
that are more flexible and forgiving. Our universal conscious-
ness is awakening.

Final Thoughts

In the seclusion of our private spaces — our bedrooms and
baths — decisions about whether or not to install phones,
message centers, TVs, computers, and other accoutrements of
daily life will have a considerable impact upon how we feel
each day — and at night as well. Perhaps the best choice is to
leave these modern functions to the other rooms in which we
live our hectic, overscheduled, and wonderful lives, preserving
our bedrooms and bathrooms for the true luxury of repose.

Even small adjustments to space and light can transform a bedroom or bath.

ABOVE Louvered windows and a soaring ceiling capture space and light, bringing architectural drama to a soothing style.
Design: Patkau Architects, Inc.

OPPOSITE Strong horizontal and vertical forms contrast with the sweeping curve of the shower wall. Colors, textures, and materials are borrowed from nature, and privacy is provided by a little garden wall.
Design: Clodagh

While most rooms start with four walls, a ceiling, and a floor, there is infinite variety in the ways these six planes can be pierced, folded, pleated, bent, tucked, curved, expanded, and contracted. The three-dimensional volume of space and light that results from those manipulations will form the foundation of your bedroom or bath — the architectural shell inside which all your other design ideas will be brought together. It is wise, therefore, to look first to your architecture to exploit its potential for increasing the beauty of the rooms you are planning. Major exterior changes, and even modest adjustments to interior architecture, can have a profound impact on your design.

On the following pages, we will look up, down, over, under, around, and through that simple boxlike shape with which every beautiful bedroom and bathroom begins.

nine

raw space

ABOVE A floating wall with two rectangular cutouts defines a closet behind and a small bath inside.
Design: Ruhl Walker Architects

LEFT French doors artfully separate the sleeping and sitting areas in this lovely traditional setting without interrupting the visual flow.

BELOW Heavy with history, a tapestry hangs over a sheer glass portal to the balcony. The effect is both mysterious and sensual.
Design: Clodagh

Every beautiful room deserves to make an entrance. To maximize the design potential inside your room, first examine the outside: the corridors, archways, doorcases, anterooms, stairs, landings, porches, and portals. These all-important in-between spaces have incredible power to captivate, intrigue, and excite curiosity.

You may prefer an entryway that makes a gentle transition from room to room, or one that provides a jolting surprise. In either case, the choice you make here, in the doorway, will set the tone for everything that lies ahead.

When remodeling or renovating, one sure road to success is to heed the clues provided by your home. Consistent repetition of the primary patterns of your existing architecture creates a reassuring sense of permanence, adding stature even to understated styles.

BELOW Suspended from steel beams, two perpendicular sliding panels meet in the corner to enclose a loft bedroom.
Design: Jeffrey King and Mosher, Dolan, Cataldo & Kelly

RIGHT This handsome Arts and Crafts–style doorway pays homage to its companion, an original Stickley bookcase.
Design: Ken Zawislak and Carol Grant

Think of an entryway as a picture frame for your room. Foyers, galleries, arches, corridors, and stairways will add pronounced dignity and interest to a bed or bath design. When lined with shelves, or furnished with a settee, window seat, or desk, they can be functional as well as beautiful. Pocket doors and openings without doors tend to draw less attention to themselves while maximizing the space within the rooms. Extra-wide doors on pivot hinges, double doors, Dutch doors, doors camouflaged behind bookcases or artwork, decorative screens, flat panels of fabric, and curtains over portals are among the many handsome options.

Because doorways dictate where and how we move through space, proper placement is as important as aesthetics. Carefully analyze traffic patterns and how your rooms relate to one another and to the outdoors. And, of course, patios, porches, and balconies, like any other rooms, deserve entryways that suit their function and enhance their style.

RIGHT Beveled glass doors add sparkle to the richly detailed doorcase that ceremoniously connects this dressing room to the master bedroom. All of the woodwork is faux-painted and finished with an ochre glaze to resemble ancient plaster walls.
Design: William Draper and Randall Sisk

LEFT The exquisite craftsmanship, beautiful grain, and rich color of this extraordinary arched door provide a perfect introduction to a lovely powder room.
Design: Design Specifications, Inc.

Though insubstantial as air, light creates
architecture just as surely as any solid form. Without the play
of light and shadow, curves flatten out, rich details are
obscured, and solid shapes virtually disappear.

Absent sufficient illumination, even the most glorious
design will be blunted. Windows, skylights, and glazed doors
and panels in all their many incarnations — clerestory, conserva-
tory, porthole, stained- or art-glass, transparent or translucent,
to name just a few — add architectural richness as well as light.

In addition to adequate general light, issues of proper task
lighting and effective accent lighting are more important to
fine design than ever before. Interior designers and architects
have discovered the merit of consulting with lighting design
specialists in order to make best use of new technologies.
Lighting plans are now designed in layers and zones

throughout a room with subtlety and sophistication.
Chandeliers, lamps, sconces, track, recessed and cove lighting,
and even artificially illuminated faux windows and skylights,
are just some of the choices available today.

Reflective surfaces such as mirrors, highly polished metals
and stones, and glossy ceramic tile glazes, as well as more
subtly reflective surfaces such as satin-finished stainless steel
and nickel, can augment the sense of light.

ABOVE LEFT Glass blocks in an
exterior wall eliminate the need for
window coverings, while glass blocks
in an interior shower wall turn the
shower's ceiling light into a night-
light for the bedroom.
Design: CCBG Architects, Inc.

ABOVE RIGHT Indoors and
outdoors merge as sun pours into
this bathroom from a skylight inside
the shower. A vanity floats in front
of floor-to-ceiling windows, keeping
the room airy and open.
Design: Maxine Snider

There is no light more magnetic than firelight. And fireplaces, with their magical promise of that lovely light and their inherent structural authority, will enhance any bed or bath design. Though no longer a practical necessity, the fireplace is architecturally and aesthetically as powerful as ever.

In addition to wood-burning fireplaces, gas, electric, and even holographic fireplaces offer intriguing design possibilities. But whether decorated with plants or candles or left entirely unornamented, a fireplace is a natural focal point that can anchor a room.

The unique bathroom design shown at right was once a spare bedroom in a run-down Boston rooming house. With a lavish sense of style and an eye for the potential of the space, the new owner and her architect raised the old hearth rather than cover it over as they had originally planned when they decided to use the room as the master bath. With casework to match the existing architecture, they enclosed the soaking tub between a shoulder-high linen cabinet and a monolithic picture-frame mantel of rose marble. The newly built cabinets on the far wall continue the handsome Greek Revival style of the suite, and the strength of this interior architecture is supplemented by the luxury of natural light from two large windows.

ABOVE In this bathroom converted from a rooming-house bedroom, the fireplace was raised to accommodate a deep tub, and enclosed in a marble surround with a massive lintel to provide a sense of monumentality.
Design: Duckham + McDougal Architects

RIGHT A low, mirrored frieze that wraps around the room (even through the glass shower) accentuates the dynamic horizontality of this design, which places the tub and shower atop two steps. Bands of light yellow Parisian sandstone inlaid with Carrara marble establish a grid upon which the room was patterned.
Design: Emanuela Frattini Magnusson

Ceiling architecture has a dramatic impact on the feeling of a room. Raising the ceiling even a foot, or incorporating coffers, vaults, or beams, will add dimension and texture that completely alter a room.

Floors, like ceilings, can be raised, lowered, ramped, stepped, pierced, and decorated, significantly affecting the feeling of a room by the way they define space. The flow or shift of materials from area to area will set or eliminate boundaries, and even the simple decision to lay tiles on a diagonal grid can make a room seem wider.

RIGHT This guest bedroom for grandchildren has its own play loft, accessed by a magical staircase embellished with drawers, cubbies, and one tread that extends back to form a desk. On the other side of the loft, a secret passageway and ladder lead down into another guest room.
Design: Lyman Perry Architects, Ltd.

LEFT Attics reach new heights when exploited for their full potential. This one, in a 1743 farmhouse, is now a guest room. The original beams, floorboards, and rough stone flue, along with the embracing arms of the new queen-sized bed, create a feeling of cozy protection. A nineteenth-century Irish side chair, classic blue-and-white ticking, and layers of personal treasures add more history and charm.
Design: Robert Couturier

LEFT The sweeping arch of this beamed ceiling leads the eye to a spectacular view of a two-acre pond. A little balcony brings nature even closer.
Design: Stamberg Aferiat Architecture

BELOW Mirrors framing a clerestory window create the illusion of even more light and space and achieve a captivating interplay between reflection and transparency.
Design: Mojo Stumer Associates

OPPOSITE An intelligently designed sculptural element separates the bedroom and bathroom, displays art, and serves as headboard, cabinet, and bedside table. The integrated bed is perfectly positioned for a view of the backyard garden.
Design: Brayton & Hughes Design Studio

Bedrooms and baths can also be defined in unique and innovative ways with versatile interior architectural elements such as half walls, partitions, islands, peninsulas, archways, and cabinetry. Niches and alcoves can add depth and interest.

LEFT Five zones of activity encircle a ring of flowers and shells: his-and-her pedestal sinks on either side of freestanding cabinetry, the tub in a bay under a cathedral ceiling, the doorless shower, and a seating area. **Design: Lyman Perry Architects, Ltd.**

LEFT A walk-in closet was built under the eaves on the bedroom side of this attic suite. A bench in the steam shower sits under the eaves on the bathroom side.
Design: William and Colette Rodon Hornof

BELOW Tumbled marble tiles, a polished marble slab, cherry-stained cabinets, sheets of satin-etched glass, and three tones of paint are layered to create a waterlike, rippling effect.
Design: William and Colette Rodon Hornof

In the suite shown on this page, a sculptural partition, stepped to follow the pitch of the roofline, solved all the problems presented by a third-story attic space. Without interrupting the dramatic ceiling planes, blocking any of the three new skylights, or constricting the circulation of traffic or airflow, the partition separates the bedroom from the bathroom, serves functionally to house the vanity and provide storage, and transmits light through translucent glass panels and a three-tiered medicine cabinet.

Conceived for "sleeping only," this design was inspired by the gentle, rippling motion of a stone tossed into water. The space is sculpted with several muted hues and curving masses and planes. Tones of creamy gray taupe and mauve deepen as they move away from the bed, accentuating the concentric layering of complementary and contrasting materials. Together, the form and color evoke a restful feeling. The sophistication of the concept is underscored by subtleties such as arched feet on the vanity, a round vessel sink, and an under-counter towel bar.

OPPOSITE The architecture of this
shower enclosure partitions the
toilet area in a niche of its own,
while the step at the back of the
bathroom sets the tub apart.
Design: Weisz + Yoes Studio

Because the architectural shell you are creating
will have an impact on every other decision you make, here are
two rules to remember:

First, think contextually. Your new room should be framed
within the context of the spaces around it: your home, your
property, the neighborhood, and the region. Like a set of
Russian Matryoshka dolls, all the pieces of your design must
nest comfortably, one inside the other.

ABOVE A powder-coated
aluminum and milk-glass partition
with integrated sink separates
the bedroom from the bathroom
while keeping this small space
wide open and easy to access.
Design: The Wiseman Group and Scott Williams

RIGHT A rhythmically paneled
niche embraces a bureau, lending
structure as well as ample
breathing room to the piece's
well-proportioned good looks.
Design: Maxine Snider

Second, evaluate every spatial option with inch-by-inch attention to detail. Visionary ideas grow from shrewd scrutiny of available space. Here are a few guidelines.

➢ When searching for more room, examine every interior space you see — closets, pantries, halls, bays, staircases, basements, and attics. Is there an unnecessary doorway that should become a closet? Then look for hidden spaces — ceilings and floors that may have been raised or lowered, or windows that may have been covered over. Are there ducts, radiators, or waste lines that can be eliminated or moved, or mechanical shafts or load-bearing columns that can be narrowed?

➢ Determine which walls are structural, and which can be moved or eliminated.

➢ Evaluate your property. Can you borrow space from a garden or porch? Is there a view that you could be enjoying from your new bedroom, or from the tub?

LEFT Extra closet space defines an
extra-cozy sleeping space.
Design: Nancy Mullan

➤ While examining the natural light, consider the room's
orientation to the sun. Does the exposure take advantage
of the morning light, or capture the sunset?

➤ Think about the electrical wiring you'll need for general,
task, and accent lighting, as well as the wiring and outlets
necessary for computers, telephones, and media compo-
nents. What is — and what is not — inside the ceiling,
under the floor, and behind the walls? Are the plumbing,
air-conditioning, and heating adequate and up-to-date?

RIGHT A marble tub is
cocooned behind a pearwood
vanity, making beautiful use of all
the available space.
Design: Emanuela Frattini Magnusson

Final Thoughts

I like to think of the architectural shell of a room as having a
life of its own, separate and distinct from the bedroom, bath,
or powder room that it will hold. If the six elevations — four
walls, a floor, and a ceiling — are right, then you may proceed
with confidence as you make all the design decisions ahead.

From additions as simple and affordable as window boxes
and crown moldings to those which are far more elaborate and
expensive, such as vaulted ceilings, fireplaces, and formal
colonnades, investments in architecture are certain to heighten
the impact of every other element of your bed and bath design
with their enduring beauty.

In, through, and around rooms, floor plans serve aesthetic as well as practical needs.

ABOVE Backlit metal-and-glass doors (to the gym on one side and the laundry room on the other) illuminate this elegant hallway to the master suite.

OPPOSITE A large nineteenth-century Venetian mirror hangs above the original 1920s fireplace in the gracious bedroom lounging area.
Design: Scott Himmel, Architect P.C.

for many of us, floor plans are like maps and charts, tools we would just as soon leave in the hands of navigational experts — our architects, designers, and engineers. Abstract shapes drawn on large rolls of paper lack the immediacy of swatches of gorgeous fabrics or samples of stone and tile. But no bed or bath design is independent of the floor plan. Now that we have considered the importance of function and raw space, let's coordinate the two with plans that fit all your ideas into place, work efficiently, and provide maximum comfort.

Whether you're coordinating two small rooms or an elaborate suite, the designs that follow will get you thinking about space in new ways. Each achieves an easy compatibility between function and aesthetics.

ten

floor plan

OPPOSITE LEFT Architectural detailing, such as the coffered ceiling and the glass-shelved niche for the bed, is the hallmark of this scheme.
Design: Ken Zawislak and Carol Grant

OPPOSITE RIGHT Tramp art from the 1920s, a stool by Viennese designer Josef Hoffmann with vintage fabric, French glass, ceramics, and a cut-and-sewn lithograph over the tub complement the golden tones in the slate and wood.
Design: Ken Zawislak and Carol Grant

LEFT The breakthrough idea in this suite was to break through . . . to the unheated attic space above. His office, with three skylights, is now the architectural highlight of the plan. The open bookcases built along a "gangplank" high above the bed add interest and also support the roof.
Design: Ken Zawislak and Carol Grant

Occupying the entire second story and attic of a
handsome Dutch colonial home, this suite was made for "all
the things we need to see, experience, touch, and have around
us every day." In order to capture much-needed space and
light, three small bedrooms and a bath were reconfigured.
And as one idea led to another, a dark, cramped attic was
transformed into an open, light-filled loft.

Sitting at the top of the main staircase are the master bathroom, her office, and the master bedroom with its interior loft
(which is his office). Preferring the traditional approach, in which
separate rooms serve separate functions, these homeowners deliberately chose not to integrate the master bath into their bedroom.
Placing it across the staircase landing with an independent
entrance has conveniently made the bathroom easy to share with
overnight visitors when her office is used as a guest bedroom.

In addition to flexibly accommodating a busy lifestyle, this
floor plan provides ample opportunities for displaying the fine
craftsmanship and careful attention to architectural and decorative detail that characterize this suite. In homage to the early
modernist architect and designer Charles Rennie Mackintosh,
architect Ken Zawislak designed and hand-built all of this
extraordinary woodwork himself. The three pairs of quarter-
sawn oak and frosted glass doors, accented with hand-
hammered copper pulls, not only divide rooms; they also
proudly announce the influence of the Arts and Crafts move-
ment of the early twentieth century. Elements used to define
the interior spaces, such as the railings, the ledge above the
bed (which serves as a narrow gallery for bookcases), and
other freestanding pieces and built-in cabinets, harmoniously
repeat the central motif. In a house with little available wall
space, these rooms provide much-needed places to display
the owners' treasured collections of lithography, tramp art,
photography, textiles, and wall-hung ceramics.

Beautiful and functional rooms such as these quickly teach
us that a good floor plan is so much more than just a set of
blue lines on a large sheet of paper.

Faced with a 20 x 75-foot tunnel of raw space with windows only at each end, architect Will Ruhl designed a floor plan for this Boston loft that would provide a feeling of openness, make the best use of the available light, and function flexibly. Placing the master suite and a guest bedroom at opposite ends of the apartment had several practical as well as aesthetic advantages. Both bedrooms now enjoy natural light and city views, and each room can be easily partitioned for privacy or opened for parties.

Using an interconnecting series of horizontal and vertical planes, both bedroom spaces were proportioned on a more intimate scale, softening the high-tech, industrial feeling of the loft. Concrete floors were covered with wood and the overhead grid of beams was framed in wallboard. Exposed pipes, sprinklers, and ducts were hidden and recessed lights were installed in new, lower ceiling structures.

LEFT Two contrasting vessel sinks add double function and personality to the bath. The lighting fixtures above the mirror pivot and telescope, further customizing the room.
Design: Ruhl Walker Architects

The master bath, built on a raised platform to accommodate the plumbing, has a sunken tub under the window, and the vanity island — with an open double shower behind — creates a circular traffic pattern. Continuing the soft tones that run throughout the loft, this room is sheathed in a highly textured, fossilized gray-green limestone accented by marble with white and gray veining. The hanging fixture — shaped like a fuchsia blossom — adds a splash of frivolity, and everywhere the muted tones and clean lines of the architecture quietly embrace the collection of contemporary art and furniture.

LEFT The guest bedroom is closed off with a movable wall that slides along tracks in the ceiling and floor. When the sliding wall is open, the guest room becomes part of the living room. The wooden chaise, with a view of the park (and large storage drawers beneath), was sculpted to fit the homeowner perfectly.
Design: Ruhl Walker Architects

RIGHT An inset mirror suspended above the etched-glass vessel sink is flanked by sconces of mahogany and steel designed with space-age flair. This guest room bath is also the central powder room of the apartment.
Design: Ruhl Walker Architects

There is a dynamic architectural interplay
between open and closed volumes in this floor plan. Unlike a more traditional layout in which the master suite is separated from the rest of the home, architect Michael Gelick's design floats a bedroom sitting area above the living and dining rooms on an open loft/bridge that boldly traverses the second-story space.

There is a cocoonlike sense of enclosure when one is sitting in the loft. The narrow room, accented by the custom TV cabinet and warmed by a zinc-covered fireplace, fine art, and antiques, has the same intimacy as the rest of the bedroom suite. But when you are on your feet, everything shifts dramatically. All at once, there is breathtaking space and light, and private space turns public. The loft joins with the bedroom, dressing room, master bath, and library (not shown) to complete the suite.

ABOVE This bridge above the living and dining spaces holds the sitting area for the master bedroom. The striking circular TV cabinet, in warm, honey-colored anigre (an African hardwood), bursts from the soft gray-green bridge like a bud on a branch.
Design: Michael Gelick

LEFT Built-in cabinets and the bed in the master bedroom are angled inward, leading the eye to the panoramic forest view and expanding the room's open relationship to nature.
Design: Michael Gelick

RIGHT In the sitting area, a natural palette complements the pure geometry of the zinc-clad fireplace.
Design: Michael Gelick

BELOW From the central corridor of the master suite, one passes through the dressing room into the master bathroom, where nature's beauty is — quite literally — reflected in the design.
Design: Michael Gelick

The walls and floor of the bathroom are clad in French limestone in an 8 x 16-inch running bond pattern, with limestone slabs on the vanity top and surrounding the tub. Lit with a combination of incandescent and fluorescent lamps, the room is also flooded with natural light from the window wall above the whirlpool tub. The dressing room just outside the bathroom is lined with custom cabinetry of anigrewood.

In the bedroom, elliptical bedside tables on wheels hold reading lamps, telephones, clock radios, and audio headsets for stereo and TV. A bedside panel controls the lighting, intercom, security system, and electrically powered blackout shades and draperies. The angled wall of cabinetry, built of anigre and frameless fiber-laminated glass, adds a golden glow.

Artful interior architecture and furniture arrangement combine to pack a lot of function into this compact space created by architect Trevor Abramson and interior designer Wendi Anton.

In the bedroom, a large four-poster bed — almost a room within a room — and tray ceiling add visual interest by subtly redefining a predictable rectangular space. The desk area gets its charm from a wall of leaded windows framed by shades and curtains. At the end of the bed, a seating area facing built-in cabinets is designed for reading and watching TV. Perfectly proportioned for the room, the ottoman (with hidden storage) and chairs continue the soft, plush feeling of the bedding but are set apart by their deeper color.

The delicately scaled master bath is flooded with light from multiple windows and a pyramid-shaped skylight in the shower. With its lowered ceiling, inset medicine cabinet, and individually framed mirrors and cabinets of varying heights, it projects a sense of intimacy. The creamy palette is brought to life with textured marble slabs and tile, ogee edging, and handsome moldings throughout the room. The steam shower at the end of the bathroom adds architectural interest along with spa-like comfort.

A private getaway for parents of a young, active family, this lovely suite successfully delivers the harmony and tranquillity for which it was designed.

OPPOSITE Bamboo and cane add the authentic flavor of Balinese styling to this bedroom.
Design: Abramson Teiger Architects and Wendi Anton

RIGHT A 1940s alabaster chandelier casts an ochre glow and tiny beads of crystal sparkle on the lampshades and window blinds. Antique candlesticks provide a touch of romance. Inside the shower are a built-in bench and a pretty window.
Design: Abramson Teiger Architects and Wendi Anton

LEFT Long before these homeowners even dreamed of moving west, they fell in love with the color and curves of this bamboo bed. Transported across the country, it has found its perfect home, and seems to have inspired the rounded plaster walls, deep sienna color, and curving circulation pattern of the suite.
Design: Lash McDaniel

BELOW A grid of bamboo on a circular recess over the tub creates a windowlike effect. Wood shutters and custom-designed tile on the countertops add more texture and pattern.
Design: Lash McDaniel

It only took a short weekend trip for the desert to cast its spell on these Scottsdale, Arizona, homeowners. Drawn to all the natural wonder of the Southwest, they combined the terra-cotta glow of the desert earth and sun with the roughness of adobe-style walls in their master suite. The rich color works well with the rounded walls and the circular floor plan to give these rooms a sheltering warmth — the feeling of a well-protected enclave. These transplanted city dwellers brought with them a sophisticated collection of art and artifacts acquired over years of travel, including their unique bent-bamboo bed.

One key to their design success was the ample time invested in planning. According to architect Lash McDaniel, "The most important thing is to find out who the clients are and to build up architectural layers around how they live and move." This floor plan does just that. The shared bathroom is located behind the bed, with separate entrances for husband and wife, each with its own walk-in closet and vanity area. In the bedroom, bamboo sliding doors open onto a patio and reveal a breathtaking view of the mountains.

Here's a checklist of ideas to keep in mind as you develop the perfect floor plan:

➤ When we begin remodeling, there is a natural tendency to let the existing floor plan dominate our thinking. Even the most awkward floor plan has an authority and sense of permanence that are difficult to contradict. It takes foresight and confidence to alter an existing arrangement of spaces. Yet successful remodeling requires rethinking all the architectural assumptions presented by your current space. A seemingly wild extravagance, such as moving the bathroom to the opposite side of the suite or installing a window or skylight in a walk-in closet, can be the idea that totally transforms a design. Just keep in mind that electrical wiring and plumbing are easier to reroute than wastewater drains and outside vents.

➤ Bed and bath suites can be divided into separate rooms for sleeping, studying, exercising, dressing, grooming, and bathing. They may include a private water closet, sauna, steam shower, hot tub, laundry, and even a kitchen. But the same functional result can be achieved in an open plan   a series of interrelated areas within a single room. So if you're not planning to build or tear down walls or otherwise reconfigure the raw space of your existing bed or bath, consider these options for enhancing your plan:

◎ Employ architectural elements, such as columns and arches, half walls, and partitions to separate spaces or open them up to one another.

◎ Use furniture groupings to define areas within your floor plan.

◎ Incorporate platforms, steps, area rugs, and variant flooring materials to visually partition an open space. Changes in the ceiling plane can have the same impact. Without the cost of a new ceiling or roof, you can suspend a row of pendant lights, a shelf, a mirror, or a glazed cabinet from the ceiling over a table or island to visually define separate areas.

➤ Because storage is so important in bedrooms and bathrooms, make a detailed inventory of everything you ll be keeping there: linens, towels, grooming aids, medicines, cleaning supplies, clothing, shoes, accessories, suitcases, books . . . everything. Armed with this information, you ll be able to plan your new storage space with an enlightened perspective on what you have, what you use, and where it should go. You won t have to guess about the number of drawers you ll need next to the bed or in the makeup table. You may also find that it s time to say good-bye to that pair of jeans you were sure you d fit into again one day or that Hawaiian shirt you bought that s been sitting in your closet.

➤ Consider departing from predictable arrangements of bathroom cabinetry. Innovations such as island vanities (some with double sinks placed back-to-back), a grooming center under a window in a walk-in closet (perhaps equipped with a small sink), or makeup table on wheels can simultaneously enhance function and design.

➤ One of the best ways to improve a floor plan is to make the most of the sight line : what you see the moment you enter the room. A floor plan can be transformed simply by positioning the entry to create an exciting first impression a window that brings in a beautiful vista, a lovely alcove, or an antique armoire, rather than a blank wall.

➤ While you may not presently use a wheelchair or have other special physical needs, it might nevertheless be wise to plan now for such eventualities. There may come a time when wider doorways, thresholds that are flush to the floor, and other accommodations you build today will be cherished for more than just their aesthetic appeal.

RIGHT AND BELOW Glass clerestory windows above the stone wall are echoed on the interior walls, providing architectural continuity.
Design: Adolfo Perez, Architect

Old stone walls are a familiar sight on the New England landscape. In this extraordinary home, the robust, primitive beauty of stone is illuminated by integrated up-and-down lights and set in a dramatic radial shape to tell a contemporary story.

With a glass curtain wall on the ocean side of the house and a curved ceiling floating over clerestory windows, architect Adolfo Perez created a floor plan that maintains this same spectacular sense of openness throughout the master suite. The bedroom, two dressing rooms, the master bath, a sauna, and a whirlpool are all arranged along a sweeping corridor paved with camel-colored carpeting.

Using a controlled neutral palette enlivened by reddish mahogany and reflective burnished copper, Perez artfully continued the arc motif of the stone wall to the interior architecture of the suite. The most stunning example is the massive sculptural headboard with its soaring fan shape (curved on the back, but flat on the bedside and on top). The repetitive, cathedral-patterned graining of the South American mahogany brings deep, earthy detail to the purity of this modern form.

Final Thoughts

Because the eye is readily drawn to vivacious colors, patterns, textures, and forms, floor plans can easily go unnoticed. That's probably because the better they work, the less obtrusive they are in supporting the life and design of your rooms. Therefore, as you collect new ideas, pay careful and deliberate attention to the layout of your favorite rooms. For just under the lovely surfaces, you're sure to discover an intelligence and logic that account for much of the beauty you see and feel.

There is no defense against the power of beauty... and style brings it home.

eleven
style

Once upon a time, fine design was a privilege of the few. And styles were often rigid, following strict rules. But today, great design is widely accessible and diverse. Your personal style may follow historical precedent, or be utterly innovative. You may draw inspiration from antiquity, or from cutting-edge technology. Though spanking-new ideas are rare, your creative spirit is quite apt to discover a new combination of ideas that is uniquely your own.

Searching for style requires curiosity, an open mind, and even some risk taking, and is sure to be a wonderful adventure. This chapter features many distinctive styles to stimulate your imagination. Let's start in the powder room, that wonderful little design laboratory where big ideas often begin.

ABOVE LEFT Referencing French furniture of the 1940s, this English sycamore vanity balances gracefully on splayed legs. Its parchment doors are detailed with crystal ball knobs and tiny keyholes. The wall of onyx mosaic, glistening with light, epitomizes the textural complexity of this monochromatic scheme.
Design: M (Group)

ABOVE RIGHT The dramatic styling of this powder room illustrates the collaborative power of strong geometric forms and neutral colors. The deep architectural angularity, bare lightbulb, and stainless steel vessel sink (with a hose for a drain) are perfect partners for the earth tones of the putty-colored plaster walls — decisively proving that beige need never be boring!
Design: Clodagh

ABOVE LEFT This old-world style begins with an antique Austrian chest that was retrofitted as a washstand. Dark walls accented by a pair of sconces and a leaded art-glass exterior window contrast with the textured stone floor.
Design: Barbara Houston

ABOVE RIGHT Hand-sculpted adobe walls form niches and alcoves for treasured antiques and art in this powder room designed to reflect the desert's own beauty. Dark, rough-textured plaster imparts a cavelike feeling, while a sink and mirror fashioned from weathered vessels create a southwestern sophistication.
Design: Lash McDaniel

ABOVE LEFT A green glass vessel sink balances on a cone of stainless steel in a dappled marble cube. Two perpendicular planes of glass combine to create a minimal vanity, while a baton of milky glass and chrome anchors the design.
Design: Sura Malaga-Strachan

ABOVE RIGHT Inspired by the artistry of Charles Rennie Mackintosh, this powder room introduces guests to design themes that run throughout the home. Stained glass with a rose motif is the background for collectibles that celebrate handcraftsmanship and natural colors and textures.
Design: Ken Zawislak and Carol Grant

ABOVE LEFT A tiny powder room makes a decisive design statement. The effect is dramatic when a few simple gray stones are tossed into the richly textured palette of natural materials that was employed throughout this home.
Design: Peter Sollogub and Maho Abe

ABOVE RIGHT Framed by French-polished Cuban mahogany, an Art Deco commode is topped with an integrated stone sink and counter. This glamorous decor is illuminated by Louis Comfort Tiffany sconces and an overhead brass fixture.
Design: M (Group)

ABOVE LEFT With the plumbing tucked unobtrusively into the corner, this vanity has the look of a classic entry table one would expect to find in a traditional foyer. The picture-framed mirror, dark-shaded table lamp, and crystal and silver appointments complete the effect, offering a gracious welcome to guests.
Design: Gene Pindzia

ABOVE RIGHT This room, a study in contrasts, is dominated by the impressive Z-shaped black apron that frames the mirror. The contemporary style unites sheer planes of geometry reminiscent of the Bauhaus and robust materials from regional New England architecture.
Design: Adolfo Perez, Architect

ABOVE LEFT A sink sculpted from translucent onyx, a tube of light, and a single wall-mounted fixture confirm the extraordinary power of simple geometry and beautiful natural materials.
Design: Minsuk Cho and James Slade

ABOVE RIGHT This composition has roots in New England's proud architectural heritage, calling to mind the grand summer homes of the 1930s. The frosted-glass doors, painstakingly salvaged from an old butler's pantry near the kitchen, contribute a Swedish flavor first introduced by the original owners.
Design: Erica Broberg Architect

The French are well known for living life with exceptional charm and for paying careful attention to the details of every daily event. There is clearly a sweet, French country flavor in this three-room master suite in the home of a young and busy family with two children and a dog. The attention to detail is equally evident.

Moving into this new and much larger home, the lady of the house was determined not to forfeit the understated beauty of the family's previous residence. By attending first to the architectural shell — adding beams in the sitting room and reworking all the wood ceilings with a distressed finish — designer Donna Livingston was able to soften the dramatic angles of the high-pitched ceiling. The large rooms were brought down to a more comfortable, embracing scale without sacrificing any of their natural light or luxurious openness.

In the bedroom, the custom-designed four-poster bed with vintage linens is paired with an antique armoire in the corner that stylishly hides the TV and stereo system. The handmade quilt from West Virginia is just one of many pieces of American folk art throughout the home, where art and antiques are mixed freely with newer pieces and custom-made cabinetry. The fabulous view of the gardens joins with the golds and muted pastels of the floral draperies and valance to enhance the warmth and intimacy of this lovely space.

A bay of windows and a long skylight flood the master bathroom with sunshine that reflects off mirrored walls and the white polished-marble floor. Floating in the treetops, this master suite has found an easy balance between casual comfort and pure luxury.

ABOVE The valance above the French doors repeats the strong horizontality of the crossbeams, effectively lowering the ceiling and adding the softness of its floral pattern to the large expanse of open window.
Design: Donna Livingston Design

LEFT The bath, with glass shower stall and a view of the treetops from the tub, is accessorized with an array of antiques — many found by the designer on her frequent trips to New Orleans.
Design: Donna Livingston Design

LEFT In accordance with Japanese tradition, this room includes one area for washing and rinsing, and a soaking tub for relaxation.
Design: Brininstool + Lynch

BELOW A wall of etched glass admits the light from the hallway windows into this space, which leads to a large walk-in closet. The mirror over the floating maple vanity is lit from the back.
Design: Brininstool + Lynch

OPPOSITE A collection of little wooden pillows from Korea sits atop the headboard, while eighteenth-century wood-block prints from Japan hang on the wall above. Linens can be stored inside the slatted bench built into the foot of the bed; a sliding shelf next to the bed holds books . . . or teacups.
Design: Brininstool + Lynch

These homeowners share a reverence for nature and a love of the understated Japanese aesthetic. The simplicity of their master suite accommodates their tastes and lifestyle perfectly.

A water closet, vanity, and walk-in clothes closet sit between the bedroom at one end of the suite and a large 7 x 14-foot shower room on the other. The floor plan provides circulation from two corridors; sun pours in through a grid of windows in the exterior corridor, while the interior corridor is lined with additional closets.

The furniture, cabinetry, doors, and window framing are all custom-designed in maple; only the matching maple soaking tub was ordered from a manufacturer. The wall-to-wall carpeting in the bedroom in a neutral gray-green harmonizes with the slate floor beyond.

Materials throughout the bedroom and the bathroom are deliberately modest. Small, deep blue tiles are set against dark slate, glass, and clear blond wood. Much of the effectiveness of this design comes from the architectural impact of the repetitive geometry of sculpted niches that augment simple rectilinear space with depth and light. Above the bed is an asymmetrical negative space that architect Brad Lynch calls an "unsoffit"; and over the closets in the inner hallway, he has carved openings that bring in light from additional hidden sources. There is an authority in these pure forms that may account for their enduring beauty.

This master bathroom and dressing room suite, designed by architect Elliott Rosenblum, takes its pristine elegance from clear lines and a controlled palette. Large book-matched panels of crotch mahogany are framed with a bead of bronze inlay, then set into standard mahogany stiles and rails and topped with a simple crown. While the moldings are a gesture to tradition, the style is a reinterpretation of the early modernism of the 1930s, evoking the mood of a vintage Paris hotel or a New York City men's club.

In the bath, the tub is fitted with European faucetry and finished with an oval ledge cut from a solid marble slab, while the marble tile floor, laid on the diagonal, is detailed with a grid and border of 1 x 1-inch mosaic tiles, adding rich textural contrast. A hint of Art Deco glamour is provided by glass-and-bronze towel bars and a chandelier and sconces of luminous onyx. The sink, poised upon glass legs with tapered bronze feet, sits under an inset backlit mirror.

The decidedly masculine decor continues in the dressing room, which also serves as a small study. This private chamber is furnished with a handsome vintage chaise with a carved swan motif, glass shelves for art, books, and family photos, and an onyx chandelier suspended from a groin-vaulted ceiling.

With urban flair and sophistication, these twenty-first-century rooms draw on the heritage of one of the twentieth century's first modernist interior designers, Jean-Michel Frank. Expressing a beauty that relies on the power of natural materials articulated with immaculate symmetry and precision, these rooms achieve a graceful balance between old and new, between then and now.

OPPOSITE The frames around both windows in this bathroom are lined with mirrored panels, so that even from the tub there is a view of Central Park. The room is also illuminated by an up-lit cove ceiling with picture-frame molding.
Design: Rosenblum Architects

ABOVE Designed for reading and enjoying music from an integrated stereo system, the dressing room conceals all clothing behind doors. The three-way mirror amplifies light from another large window in the suite, making the room appear larger.
Design: Rosenblum Architects

LEFT There is no art hung on these walls; instead, windows in the bathroom and a full wall of glass on the east side of the bedroom become picture frames for the beauty of nature.
Design: Clodagh

OPPOSITE The designer was delighted to find these Dutch doors already in place in this Pacific beach house. She added the massive stone threshold to enhance the sense of transition and simply painted the doors a bronzy green — "a good feng shui color."
Design: Clodagh

A quiet stroll away from the main house, this pavilion near the water, once used for recreation and storage, has been transformed by designer Clodagh into a second master suite — "a place for changing gears." Out here, nothing competes with the sights and sounds of nature. Constructed from nontoxic, environmentally sound materials and finished in a palette of sand tones, this retreat is poised for peace.

Final Thoughts

You may choose to renovate or innovate; your style may be an idiosyncratic mix or authentically historical. But while personal styles and circumstances vary widely, one thing holds true in every successful bed and bath design: Your style is ultimately about your understanding of who you are and how you want to live. Good design begins with self-knowledge and confidence, and is graced with your own brand of beauty.

To capture your spirit, your personal rooms require a personal touch.

ABOVE A flat-screen TV sits above the mantel, framed like a work of art.

OPPOSITE The sumptuous master bed, surrounded by elegantly upholstered walls, art, and antiques, sits on a yellow-and-celadon needlepoint carpet designed in the French style.
Design: Cullman and Kravis, Inc., and Rosenblum Architects

there comes a startling point in the creative process, as one idea is layered over another, when the elements of your design begin working together in wonderfully independent ways, making you feel that suddenly your room is designing itself. This new awareness, often accompanied by a sensation of slightly detached wonderment, is actually the result of all your preparation and diligence. Every decision now leads far more easily to the next. You begin to anticipate the rhythmic click of all the jigsaw pieces as they lock together perfectly! This is one of the greatest pleasures of designing. And the one thread that ties everything together is *you* — that special and complex conglomeration of values, tastes, history, interests, idiosyncrasies, and impulses that makes you who you are.

Here are six beautiful designs, each with its own unique style.

twelve

it's my bed and bath!

LEFT Before the renovation, this gracious bathroom had been a kitchen in the adjoining apartment. The design of the shower stall was inspired by the French display cases — *vitrines* — often seen in Parisian boutiques.
Design: Cullman and Kravis, Inc., and Rosenblum Architects

OPPOSITE TOP An elaborate acanthus-leaf crown molding over the Palladian-inspired dressing table mirror complements the delicacy of the hand-painted ceiling. Backlighting around the perimeter of the mirror is practical for grooming and gives the room a beautiful glow.
Design: Cullman and Kravis, Inc., and Rosenblum Architects

OPPOSITE BOTTOM Adjoining her bathroom (and accessible through pocket doors on both sides of the shower) is her dressing room. When the pocket doors are open, these two rooms function as one, with a 360-degree circulation pattern.
Design: Cullman and Kravis, Inc., and Rosenblum Architects

The two bathrooms, each with its own adjoining dressing room, define contemporary function with an old-world grandeur. Her bathroom, with its soft Palladian curves and hand-painted ceiling and vanity, reflects a feminine spirit. In her dressing room, under an antique nineteenth-century chandelier, everything is meticulously arranged for convenience. An ottoman for putting on shoes is also used for packing. Clothing hooks retract into a series of ornamental pilasters that flank the closets. Glass shelves for shoes and slatted, vertical compartments for purses are hidden behind the mirrored doors.

Built in newly available space from the apartment next door, this master suite addition by interior designer Elissa Cullman and architect Elliott Rosenblum transformed a wonderful New York residence into an even more spectacular home for a busy family of five. The homeowners' single requirement for the floor plan was to keep their bedroom near the children's. But after much scrutiny and several drawings, the decision was made to listen to the architecture instead, and locate the new master bedroom (see overleaf) in the former living room on the far side of the new space. Now family members gather together on the 5-square-foot chaise in the corner to watch a flat-screen TV that sits like a painting over the Robert Adam–style fireplace mantel.

Distinguished by architecture and decoration that attend to every detail, this design is as practical as it is refined. The suite includes a gym, private office, and staff office (shown on pages 106 and 110), all flanking the master gallery that leads to the central bedroom and baths.

OPPOSITE This former powder room was enlarged to become his new bath. In an extraordinary touch, the green marble in the shower and on the countertop was detailed to match the ribbon-striped mahogany paneling and cabinetry.
Design: Cullman and Kravis, Inc., and Rosenblum Architects

ABOVE His dressing room occupies space that had previously been part of the foyer in the apartment next door.
Design: Cullman and Kravis, Inc., and Rosenblum Architects

In his bathroom, the highly polished mahogany paneling is finished with vertical rope molding, mahogany grids over the vents, and an ornate crown that includes both a dental and egg-and-dart motif. The warm, woody tones of the English-inspired cabinetry are complemented by cool, green-and-white veined marble. The adjoining dressing room, accented with nineteenth-century Chinese prints, leather boxes, and an antique Swedish chest edged with brass strapping, is illuminated by a chandelier and brass wall-mounted fixtures. It reflects the same sophisticated combination of elegance and function that characterizes every aspect of this suite.

Referencing the long history of shipping between
New England and the Far East, this Nantucket master suite
by designer Price Connors of Dujardin Design Associates has
imported a certain Asian flair. Yankee simplicity and the
understatement of the Orient are woven together seamlessly,
making this a perfect place for soothing weekend retreats.

In the bathroom, classic materials and treatments have
been refined and clarified. Bead-board wainscoting is capped
with a heavy molding. Two tall glazed towers with integrated
hampers flank the tub. And a single row of dark wooden shutters (inspired by the towel bar on the tub and the rich woods
in the bedroom) counterbalances the high ceiling and gives
this room its intimate scale and warmth. In the bedroom,
center stage, is a contemporary version of the four-poster bed,
its traditional heft infused with a delicate new purity. The

8-foot posts, tapered like the masts of a ship, play their part
in a subtle nautical theme repeated throughout the suite:
A schooner sails in the seascape over the marble fireplace;
seashells rest above the mantel; and on the coffee table, the
seven-piece gilded glass assemblage glows watery blue. Under
the eaves, traditional cabinetry is combined with the sparkle of
glass shelving. Modern and antique furniture and accessories
— of bamboo, wicker, lacquer, inlaid wood, and silver leaf —
are mixed with easy flair.

The only sounds in the room (where TV was deliberately
omitted) are music from the integrated stereo and the hum of
the ceiling fan as it encourages the breeze from the ocean.
Even the colors here are quiet. The view through French doors
and past the balcony includes the harbor and the town. The
feeling is intoxicating.

OPPOSITE Elegantly tapered ebony bedposts lead the eye to the dramatic structure of the pitched roof.
Design: Dujardin Design Associates

BELOW This design owes its success in part to careful attention to nuance, such as the white marble inlay that borders the beige bathroom floor and the balanced use of rich brown tonalities throughout the suite.
Design: Dujardin Design Associates

During the ten glorious years that designer Mary
Douglas Drysdale rode grand prix dressage, she would often
leave her office in Washington, D.C., on Thursday evenings at
10 p.m. and "just drive, let go, and totally relax." In the countryside of Lancaster, Pennsylvania, she found what she calls
"the most romantic space in the world," an 1823 stone farmhouse on a scenic easement. Although the house was in terrible
condition, bringing it back to life brought Mary new ways to
measure beauty and to understand nature . . . and herself.

The house became Mary's creative laboratory. After
analyzing its structure and thoroughly researching its architectural history, she began the creation of her own, very private
paradise. Two small rooms upstairs were combined to create a
single bedroom-bathroom. Tattered wall-to-wall carpeting was
removed and the original floor underneath was repaired (using
the old-fashioned method, with patches cut from tin), hand-
sanded, and then lightly glazed. Acoustical tiles from a prior
renovation were removed, revealing dark wooden beams that
Mary stained a shade brighter. Walls were replastered, then
glazed. Adapting stencil patterns from the work of nineteenth-
century itinerant artisans, Mary delicately bordered the floors
and decorated the walls.

Every element in this design was strongly influenced by
the "rambling and rough" Pennsylvania countryside. As a
young architecture student in Paris, Mary had learned about
formalism. But years later in Pennsylvania, where she listened
to the land and to the horses, she learned about nature's
imperfections and "unorganized glory," and that the best way
to harness such beauty is often simply to let it be.

RIGHT The tall canopy under a
low ceiling makes a grand gesture,
filling the space with great gingham,
floral, and patchwork comfort.
Design: Mary Douglas Drysdale

LEFT A built-in dresser
accessorized with starburst brass
candleholders, an Amish quilt
fragment, and stenciled Shaker-style
boxes holds a portrait of one of
Mary Douglas Drysdale's beloved
horses. Delicate stenciling also
borders the floor.
Design: Mary Douglas Drysdale

ABOVE The sight line from the main entry to this highly functional bedroom suite draws the eye past the sitting area, bed, and walk-in closets, through the bathroom, and into the aspen forest beyond. Tucked behind the fireplace is a desk.
Design: Abramson Teiger Architects

Surrounded by an aspen forest and views of Mount Wilson and Mount Sunshine, this Colorado retreat was conceived as a contemporary log cabin. In place of traditional logs, architect Trevor Abramson substituted flat planks on both the interior and exterior walls, replacing the traditional heavy mortar chinking with reveals, the recessed grooves that are a hallmark of contemporary design. The mullions of the steel windows, in a color reminiscent of Frank Lloyd Wright's favorite red, are precisely aligned with the reveals, maintaining the strong horizontal motif, a theme artfully reinforced by the horizontal planes of bluestone in the fireplace, shelving, vanity, and tub surround.

In the bedroom, cool slate floors in a running bond pattern contrast with the warm reddish ceiling, which hovers over the space in a sweeping arch. Fabricated from vibrantly veined, book-matched cherrywood, the ceiling conceals motorized shades and indirect lighting. Another architectural focal point is the freestanding double-sided fireplace, designed with an aluminum-lined cherry recess for logs. The glistening stainless steel chimney cover contributes a soft oval geometry.

In the master bath, a cherry vanity, with a niche for towels, floats from wall to wall above the bluestone floor. In contrast to the soaring bedroom ceiling, here the backlit, floating ceiling gently curves down to create a sense of intimacy.

ABOVE RIGHT Cherry doors inset with lyrical panels of etched-glass aspen leaves open into the master suite from "the gallery of the forest" (which also leads to an office, studio, and darkroom). The deep bookcase was built for art books; and the top shelf makes it easy to display — and readily change — paintings and drawings.
Design: Abramson Teiger Architects

RIGHT A convex ceiling plane floats over the tub, a reversal of the vaulted bedroom ceiling. Throughout the suite, backlit ceilings add gentle illumination and enhance the sculptural quality of the architecture.
Design: Abramson Teiger Architects

(the five building blocks of bed & bath design)

RIGHT Purchased in London, this charming Victorian dressing table with dainty stenciling sits gracefully between entries to the toilet and the shower, reinforcing the exuberant symmetry of the angled beams and double skylights. With an open floor plan, the bedroom can be accessed from either side.
Design: Sandra Nunnerley Inc.

OPPOSITE This custom Shaker-style bed, inspired by a visit to the American furniture collection at the Winterthur Museum in Delaware, has delicately feminine lines and a headboard that suggests a smile.
Design: Sandra Nunnerley Inc.

In the Green Mountains of Woodstock, Vermont, a young New York couple found an old house that would be a perfect place for weekend vacations. A renovation/restoration was planned to accommodate their growing family, make room for guests, and give them a private, second-story master suite hideaway.

Upstairs, the existing ceiling was removed, large skylights were installed, and vintage beams (found locally) were added for decorative effect. Above the crossbeams, designer Sandra Nunnerley placed V-shaped diagonal beams. Echoing the sharp angles of the roof, their powerful symmetry and rugged surfaces transformed the space.

To graciously accommodate the homeowners' collection of modern art, Nunnerley worked in the Shaker style, its simple lines and materials complementing both the rural architecture of the house and the urban sophistication of the art. Wild ducks on the chair and ottoman add a bit of nostalgia and whimsy.

There is a lilting energy in this master suite design, a light-hearted mix of elements that range from antique to modern.

The tradition of the four-poster bed has been elegantly interpreted with a fresh, contemporary attitude and just a touch of gilding.
Design: Maxine Snider

This personal retreat is rooted in old-world and Early American styling; however, the elements are combined with a contemporary sensibility that deliberately exposes the forms and bathes the entire room in open space and ample light.

The decision by designer Maxine Snider not to use carpeting or a rug draws attention to the clean, spare elevations of the architecture and contributes a peaceful clarity to the decor. Candlelight and light-reflecting white Italian linens combine with natural sunshine to coax out the biscuit tones of the cashmere, wool, and waffle-woven textiles. Dried hydrangea hangs from one of the nickel-and-mirror sconces, and little plants introduce another natural element. Electronics were omitted from a room meant only for a good night's sleep.

Final Thoughts

My favorite room is any room that holds the life-spirit of the people who live in it. These rooms have a heartbeat that we sense the moment we enter them, even if no one is there. Somehow our bedrooms and baths — these mute and inanimate constructions — reflect our lives. They have the power to make us relive the past, and to help us prepare for the future.

It seems that as we design, we ignite a spark of life in the walls and all the objects with which we choose to surround ourselves. From the blankets in which we wrap our newborn babies and the basins in which we bathe them, to the rooms we design so many years later to welcome our grandchildren for weekend visits, there is life in everything. And design is a beautiful way to capture and hold on to all of it.

credits

COVER. design: Morehouse MacDonald and Associates, Inc., Lexington, MA; photograph: © Sam Gray, Boston, MA

FRONT MATTER. p. 1, design: Clodagh, New York, NY; photograph: © Daniel Aubry, New York, NY; p. 2, design: Lyman Perry Architects, Ltd., Berwyn, PA; photograph: Jack Weinhold, Nantucket, MA; p. 6, top row: (left) design: Lyman Perry Architects, Ltd., Berwyn, PA; photograph: Jack Weinhold, Nantucket, MA; (middle) design: Clodagh, New York, NY; photograph: © Daniel Aubry, New York, NY; (right) design: Sandra Nunnerley Inc., New York, NY; photograph: Grant Mudford, Sydney, Australia; middle row: (left) design: Whitney Stewart Interior Design, Bethesda, MD; photograph: © Walter Smalling, Jr.,Washington D.C.; (middle) design: William and Colette Rodon Hornof, 2RZ Architecture, Chicago, IL; photograph: © Alan Shortall 2003, Chicago, IL; (right) design: Deborah Berke & Partners Architects L.L.P., New York, NY; photograph: © Paul Warchol, New York, NY; bottom row: (left) design: Faulding Architecture P.C., New York, NY; photograph: © Frederick Charles, Dobbs Ferry, NY; (middle) design: Andre Rothblatt, AIA, San Francisco, CA; photograph: Ken Gutmaker Photography, San Francisco, CA; (right) design: Duckham + McDougal Architects, Boston, MA; photograph: © Sam Gray, Boston, MA

INTRODUCTION. p. 8, design: Cullman and Kravis, Inc., New York, NY; photograph: © 2002 Durston Saylor, New York, NY

PRELUDE. p. 11, design: Dujardin Design Associates, Westport, CT, and Lyman Perry Architects, Ltd., Berwyn, PA; photograph: Terry Pommett Photography, Nantucket, MA

PART ONE SECTION OPENER. design: Leslie S. Saul, IIDA, AIA, Leslie Saul & Associates, Cambridge, MA; photograph: © Anton Grassl Photography, Boston, MA

CHAPTER ONE. pp. 14–15, design: Clodagh, New York, NY; photographs: © Daniel Aubry, New York, NY; p. 16, design: Sally Weston, Hingham, MA; photograph: Brian Vanden Brink, Photographer © 2003, Rockport, ME; p. 17, design: Morehouse MacDonald and Associates, Inc., Lexington, MA; photographs: © Sam Gray, Boston, MA; pp. 18–19, design: Gabellini Associates, New York, NY; photographs; © Paul Warchol, New York, NY; p. 20, design: Duckham + McDougal Architects, Boston, MA; photograph: © Sam Gray, Boston, MA; p. 21, (left) design: LOT/EK, New York, NY; photograph: © Paul Warchol, New York, NY; p. 21, (right) design: Roger Bellera, Barcelona, Spain; photograph: Jordi Miralles Sambola, Barcelona, Spain; pp. 22–23, design: Scott Himmel, Architect P.C., Chicago, IL; photographs: © Scott Frances, New York, NY; pp. 24–25, design: Sura Malaga-Strachan, SRM Design Group, Incorporated, Holmdel, NJ; photographs: Rosemary Carroll, Doylestown, PA; pp. 26–27, design: Jean Verbridge, ASID, IIDA, and Thaddeus Siemasko, AIA, Siemasko + Verbridge, Beverly, MA; photographs: © Robert Benson, Hartford, CT

CHAPTER TWO. pp. 28–29, design: Andre Rothblatt, AIA, San Francisco, CA; photographs: Ken Gutmaker Photography, San Francisco, CA; p. 30, design: Matthew Patrick Smyth, New York, NY; photograph: © Peter Margonelli, New York, NY; p. 31, design: Marmol Radziner + Associates, Los Angeles, CA, and Monica Conroy Bodell, Manhattan Beach, CA; photograph: © Benny Chan—Fotoworks, Los Angeles, CA; p. 32, design: not available; photograph: www.kaskelphoto.com, Skokie, IL; p. 33, design: Marjorie Shushan Interior Design, New York, NY; photograph: © Scott Frances, New York, NY; p. 34, (left) design: Carl D'Aquino, Francine Monaco, and Paul Laird, D'Aquino Monaco Inc., New York, NY; photograph: Christopher Hornsby, New York, NY; (right) design: Scott Himmel, Architect P.C., Chicago, IL; photograph: © Scott Frances, New York, NY; p. 35, design: Brininstool + Lynch, Chicago, IL; photograph: Padgett and Company, Chicago, IL; p. 36, (above) design: Joan Dineen, Dineen Nealy Architects L.L.P., New York, NY; photograph: Dineen Nealy Architects L.L.P., New York, NY; (below) design: William and Colette Rodon Hornof, 2RZ Architecture, Chicago, IL; photograph: © Alan Shortall 2003, Chicago, IL; p. 37, design: Clodagh, New York, NY; photograph: © Daniel Aubry, New York, NY; pp. 38–39, design: Stuart Cohen & Julie Hacker Architects, Evanston, IL; photographs: © Alan Shortall 2003, Chicago, IL; p. 40, (left) design: Faulding Architecture P.C., New York, NY; photograph: © Frederick Charles, Dobbs Ferry, NY; (right) design: Richard F. Tomlinson II, AIA, Skidmore, Owings & Merrill L.L.P., Chicago, IL; photograph: © Hedrich-Blessing, Chicago, IL; p. 41, design: Deborah Berke & Partners Architects L.L.P., New York, NY; photograph: © Paul Warchol, New York, NY

CHAPTER THREE. pp. 42–43, design: Whitney Stewart Interior Design, Bethesda, MD; photographs: © Walter Smalling, Jr., Washington D.C.; p. 45, design: Joan Dineen, Dineen Nealy Architects L.L.P., New York, NY; photograph: Dineen Nealy Architects L.L.P., New York, NY; pp. 46–47, design: Joan Halperin/Interior Design, New York, NY; photographs: © Darwin K. Davidson, Deer Isle, ME; p. 48, design: Sabrina Balsky Interior Design Inc., New York, NY; photograph: Claude Noel, Toronto, Ontario, Canada; p. 49, design: Christine Julian, Julian Kitchen Design, Chicago, IL, and Lynn Aseltine-Kolbusz, Room Service, Inc., Glen Ellyn, IL; photographs: www.kaskelphoto.com, Skokie, IL; p. 50, design: Scott Himmel, Architect P.C., Chicago, IL; photograph: Christopher Barrett © Hedrich-Blessing, Chicago, IL; p. 52, (above) design: Sally Weston, Hingham, MA; photograph: Brian Vanden Brink, Photographer © 2003, Rockport, ME; (below) design: Ivan Bercedo and Jorge Mestre, Bercedo Mestre Arquitectes, Barcelona, Spain; photograph: Jordi Miralles Sambola, Barcelona, Spain; p. 53, design: Joan Dineen, Dineen Nealy Architects L.L.P., New York, NY; photograph: Dineen Nealy Architects L.L.P., New York, NY

CHAPTER FOUR. p. 54, design: Ruhl Walker Architects, Boston, MA; photograph: Jordi Miralles Sambola, Barcelona, Spain; p. 55, design: Resolution: 4 Architecture, New York, NY; photograph: © Paul Warchol, New York, NY; p. 56, design: Brininstool + Lynch, Chicago, IL; photographs: Christopher Barrett © Hedrich-Blessing, Chicago, IL; p. 57, design: Brininstool + Lynch, Chicago, IL; photograph: Padgett and Company, Chicago, IL; p. 58, design: Bruce Bierman Design, Inc., New York, NY; photographs: © Andrew Bordwin, New York, NY; p. 59, design: Charles Gwathmey, New York, NY; photograph: © Paul Warchol, New York, NY; p. 60, design: Sabrina Balsky Interior Design Inc., New York, NY; photograph: Claude Noel, Toronto, Ontario, Canada; p. 61, (above) design: Andre Rothblatt, AIA, San Francisco, CA; photograph: Ken Gutmaker Photography, San Francisco, CA; (below) design: Jim Ross, Ross Design Group, Orlando, FL; photograph: © Everett & Soulé, Altamonte Springs, FL; p. 62, (above) design: Sally Weston, Hingham, MA; photograph: Brian Vanden Brink, Photographer © 2003, Rockport, ME; (below) design: Emilio Lopez and Monica Ribera, Lopez Ribera Arquitectes, Barcelona, Spain; photograph: Jordi Miralles Sambola, Barcelona, Spain; p. 63, design: Leslie Markman-Stern, ASID, Chicago, IL; photograph: Paul Schlismann, Deerfield, IL; p. 64, design: Sally Weston, Weston Hewitson Architects, Hingham, MA; photograph: Brian Vanden Brink, Photographer © 2003, Rockport, ME; p. 65, design: Erica Broberg Architect, East Hampton, NY; photograph: davidduncanlivingston.com, Mill Valley, CA

CHAPTER FIVE. p. 66, design: Sandra Nunnerley Inc., New York, NY; photograph: Grant Mudford, Sydney, Australia; p. 67, design: LOT/EK, New York, NY; photograph: © Paul Warchol, New York, NY; pp. 68–69, design: Alexander Gorlin Architects, New York, NY; photographs: Peter Aaron/Esto, New York, NY; p. 70, design: Ronald Bricke, Ronald Bricke & Associates, New York, NY; photographs: Michael L. Hill, New York, NY; p. 71, design: Nasrallah Fine Architectural Design, Winter Park, FL; photographs: © Everett & Soulé, Altamonte Springs, FL; p. 72, design: Joe Lehman and Martha Hatrak, Allied Member, ASID, Marlton, NJ; photograph: Rosemary Carroll, Doylestown, PA; p. 73, (above) design: Jamie Drake, Drake Design Associates, New York, NY; photograph: William Waldron, New York, NY; (below) design: Joan Halperin/Interior Design, New York, NY; photograph: © Darwin K. Davidson, Deer Isle, ME; p. 74, (above) design: Linda C. Golden, Bloomfield Hills, MI; photograph: Beth Singer, Franklin, MI; (below) design: Ray Snyder Designs, Sonoma, CA; photograph: © The Garden Spa @ MacArthur Place, Sonoma, CA; p. 75, (left) design: Clodagh, New York, NY; photograph: © Daniel Aubry, New York, NY; (right) design: William and Colette Rodon Hornof, 2RZ Architecture, Chicago, IL; photograph: © Alan Shortall 2003, Chicago, IL; p. 76, (above) design: Wendy Gardner and Stephen Gardner, New York, NY; photograph: Wendy Gardner, New York, NY; (below) design: Karen Padgett Prewitt, Quattro Canti Interiors, Charleston, SC; photograph: Leslie Wright Dow, Mooresville, NC; p. 77, design: Asfour Guzy Architects, New York, NY; photograph: © Paul Warchol, New York, NY; pp. 78–79, design: Stuart Cohen & Julie Hacker Architects, Evanston, IL, and Stephanie Wohlner Design, Highland Park, IL; photographs: Jon Miller © Hedrich-Blessing, Chicago, IL; p. 80, design: Resolution: 4 Architecture, New York, NY; photograph: © Paul Warchol, New York, NY; p. 81, design: Olson Sundberg Kundig Allen Architects, Seattle, WA, and Ted Tuttle Interior Design, Seattle, WA; photograph: © Paul Warchol, New York, NY

CHAPTER SIX. p. 82, design: Mojo Stumer Associates, Greenvale, NY; photograph: © Phillip Ennis, Bedford, NY; p. 83, design: Woodmeister Corporation, Worcester, MA; photograph: Richard Pandiscio, Providence, RI; p. 84, (left) design: Ausberg Interiors, Birmingham, MI; photograph: Beth Singer, Franklin, MI; (right) design: Michelle Pheasant Design, Inc., Monterey, CA; photograph: davidduncanlivingston.com, Mill Valley, CA; p. 85, (above) design: Laura Bohn Design Associates, New York, NY; photograph: William Waldron, New York, NY; (below) design: The Wiseman Group, San Francisco, CA, and Scott Williams, AIA, San Francisco, CA; photograph: Richard Barnes ©, San Francisco, CA; p. 86, (above) design: Leslie S. Saul, IIDA, AIA, Leslie Saul & Associates, Cambridge, MA; photograph: © Anton Grassl Photography, Boston, MA; (below) design: John Petrarca, Studio Petrarca, New York, NY; photograph: © Paul Warchol, New York, NY; p. 87, (left) design: Kendall Wilkinson Design, San Francisco, CA; photograph: davidduncanlivingston.com, Mill Valley, CA; (right) design: Cullman and Kravis, Inc., New York, NY, and John B. Murray Architects, New York, NY; photograph: Peter Peirce, New York, NY; p. 88, (above) design: Brininstool + Lynch, Chicago, IL; photograph: Padgett and Company, Chicago, IL; (below) design: Toshiko Mori Architect, New York, NY; photograph: © Paul Warchol, New York, NY; p. 89, (left) design: Erica Broberg Architect, East Hampton, NY, and Ruth Ann McSpadden, Housefitters, New York, NY; photograph: Scott W. Smith, New York, NY; (right) design: Laura Bohn Design Associates, New York, NY; photograph: Peter Margonelli, New York, NY; p. 90, (left) design: Jan Gleysteen Architects, Inc.,Wellesley, MA; photograph: © Sam Gray, Boston, MA; (right) design: Stamberg Aferiat Architecture, New York, NY; photograph: © Paul Warchol, New York, NY; p. 91, (above) design: Robinson & Shades Design Group (L. V. Shades), Tucson, AZ; photograph: Brett Drury Architectural Photography, Escondido, CA; (below) design: Scott Himmel, Architect P.C., Chicago, IL; photograph: © Scott Frances, New York, NY; p. 92, (left) design: Eddie Saunders, Saunders Design, San Francisco, CA; photograph: davidduncanlivingston.com, Mill Valley, CA; (right) design: Fox-Nahem Design, New York, NY; photograph: © Scott Frances, New York, NY; p. 93, (left) design: Alexander Gorlin Architects, New York, NY; photograph: Peter Aaron/Esto, New York, NY; (right) design: Andre Rothblatt, AIA, San Francisco, CA; photograph: Ken Gutmaker Photography, San Francisco, CA

CHAPTER SEVEN. (all) design: Peter Sollogub, Chermayeff, Sollogub and Poole, Inc., Boston, MA, and Maho Abe, ZEN Associates Inc., Sudbury, MA; photographs: Richard Mandelkorn, Lincoln, MA; additional resources: National Kitchen + Bath Association (NKBA): (800) 843–6522; American Institute of Architects (AIA): (800) 242–3837; American Society of Interior Designers (ASID): www.interiors.org

PART TWO SECTION OPENER. design: Dujardin Design Associates, Westport, CT, and Lyman Perry Architects, Ltd., Berwyn, PA; photograph: Terry Pommett Photography, Nantucket, MA

CHAPTER EIGHT. p. 106, design: Cullman and Kravis, Inc., New York, NY, and Rosenblum Architects, New York, NY; photograph: © Durston Saylor, New York, NY; p. 107, design: Stuart Cohen & Julie Hacker Architects, Evanston, IL; photograph: Jon Miller © Hedrich-Blessing, Chicago, IL; pp. 108–109, design: Bruce Bierman Design, Inc., New York, NY; photographs: © Andrew Bordwin, New York, NY; p. 110, design: Cullman and Kravis, Inc., New York, NY, and Rosenblum Architects, New York, NY; photographs: © Durston Saylor, New York, NY; p. 111, design: M (Group), New York, NY; photographs: Billy Cunningham, New York, NY; p. 112, design: Emanuela Frattini Magnusson, EFM Design & Architecture, New York, NY; photograph: David Whittaker, Toronto, Ontario, Canada; p. 113, (above) design: Clodagh, New York, NY; photograph: Keith Scott Morton, New York, NY; (below) design: Jean Verbridge, ASID, IIDA, and Thaddeus Siemasko, AIA, Siemasko + Verbridge, Beverly, MA; photograph: © Robert Benson, Hartford, CT; p. 114, (left) design: Donna Livingston Design, Los Angeles, CA; photograph: David O. Marlow, Aspen, CO; (right) design: Adolfo Perez, Architect, Newton, MA; photograph: Nick Wheeler, Weston, MA; p. 115, design: Jan Gleysteen Architects, Inc., Wellesley, MA; photograph: © Sam Gray, Boston, MA; p. 116, (left) design: Joan Halperin/Interior Design, New York, NY; photograph: © Darwin K. Davidson, Deer Isle, ME; (right) design: Jean Verbridge, ASID, IIDA, and Thaddeus Siemasko, AIA, Siemasko + Verbridge, Beverly, MA; photograph: Avanti Studios, Boston, MA; p. 117, design: Dujardin Design Associates, Westport, CT, and Lyman Perry Architects, Ltd., Berwyn, PA; photograph: Thibault Jeanson, New York, NY; p. 118, design: Jan Gleysteen Architects, Inc., Wellesley, MA; photograph: © Sam Gray, Boston, MA; p. 119, (left) design: Erica Broberg Architect, East Hampton, NY; photograph: Tria Giovan, New York, NY; p. 119, (right) design: not available; photograph: davidduncanlivingston.com, Mill Valley, CA; p. 120, design: Chelly Bloom, Chicago, IL, and Miguel A. Cruz, M.A.C. Design, Chicago, IL; photograph: Anthony May Photography, Chicago, IL; p. 121, design: Andy Newman Architect, Carpenteria, CA; photograph: davidduncanlivingston.com, Mill Valley, CA

CHAPTER NINE. p. 122, design: Patkau Architects, Inc., Vancouver, B.C., Canada; photograph: © Paul Warchol, New York, NY; p. 123, design: Clodagh, New York, NY; photograph: Keith Scott Morton, New York, NY; p. 124, design: Ruhl Walker Architects, Boston, MA; photograph: Jordi Miralles Sambola, Barcelona, Spain; p. 125, (above) design: not available; photograph: davidduncanlivingston.com, Mill Valley, CA; (below) design: Clodagh, New York, NY; photograph: © Daniel Aubry, New York, NY; p. 126, (left) design: Jeffrey King, Birmingham, MI, and Mosher, Dolan, Cataldo & Kelly, Birmingham, MI; photograph: Beth Singer, Franklin, MI; (right) design: Ken Zawislak, Royal Oak, MI, and Carol Grant, Royal Oak, MI; photograph: Beth Singer, Franklin, MI; p. 127, (left) design: Design Specifications, Inc., Maitland, FL; photograph: © Everett & Soulé, Altamonte Springs, FL; (right) design: William Draper and Randall Sisk, Holicong, PA; photograph: Beth Singer, Franklin, MI;

p. 128, design: Sally Weston, Hingham, MA; photograph: Brian Vanden Brink, Photographer © 2003, Rockport, ME; p. 129, (left) design: CCBG Architects, Inc. (Martin Ball, lead designer), Phoenix, AZ; photograph: CCBG Architects, Inc., Phoenix, AZ; (right) design: Maxine Snider, Chicago, IL; photograph: © Hedrich-Blessing, Chicago, IL; p. 130, design: Jeffrey King and Richard Ross, Birmingham, MI; photograph: Beth Singer, Franklin, MI; p. 131, (above) design: Duckham + McDougal Architects, Boston, MA; photograph: © Sam Gray, Boston, MA; (below) design: Emanuela Frattini Magnusson, EFM Design & Architecture, New York, NY; photograph: Mario Carrieri, Milan, Italy; p. 132, design: Daniel Ibars, Camallera, Spain; photograph: Jordi Miralles Sambola, Barcelona, Spain; p. 133, (left) design: Robert Couturier (originally published in *Architectural Digest*); photograph: © Scott Frances, New York, NY; (right) design: Lyman Perry Architects, Ltd., Berwyn, PA; photograph: Jeffrey Allen Photography, Nantucket, MA; p. 134, (left) design: Stamberg Aferiat Architecture (Paul Aferiat and Peter Stamberg), New York, NY; photograph: © Paul Warchol, New York, NY; (right) design: Mojo Stumer Associates, Greenvale, NY; photograph: © Jennifer Levy, New York, NY; p. 135, design: Brayton & Hughes Design Studio, San Francisco, CA; photograph: davidduncanlivingston.com, Mill Valley, CA; p. 136, design: Lyman Perry Architects, Ltd., Berwyn, PA; photograph: Jeffrey Allen Photography, Nantucket, MA; p. 137, design: William and Colette Rodon Hornof, 2RZ Architecture, Chicago, IL; photographs: © Alan Shortall 2003, Chicago, IL; p. 138, (left) design: The Wiseman Group, San Francisco, CA, and Scott Williams, AIA, San Francisco, CA; photograph: Richard Barnes ©, San Francisco, CA; (right) design: Maxine Snider, Chicago, IL; photograph: Thomas A. Nowak, Lansing, IL; p. 139, design: Weisz + Yoes Studio, New York, NY; photograph: © Paul Warchol, New York, NY; p. 140, (left) design: Nancy Mullan, ASID, CKD, New York, NY; photograph: Bill Rothschild, Wesley Hills, NY; (right) design: Emanuela Frattini Magnusson, EFM Design & Architecture, New York, NY; photograph: Gionata Xerra, Milan, Italy; p. 141, design: Maxine Snider, Chicago, IL; photograph: © Hedrich-Blessing, Chicago, IL

CHAPTER TEN. pp. 142–143, design: Scott Himmel, Architect P.C., Chicago, IL; photographs: © Scott Frances, New York, NY; pp. 144–145, design: Ken Zawislak, Royal Oak, MI, and Carol Grant, Royal Oak, MI; photographs: Beth Singer, Franklin, MI; pp. 146–147, design: Ruhl Walker Architects, Boston, MA; photographs: Jordi Miralles Sambola, Barcelona, Spain; pp. 148–149, design: Michael Gelick, Gelick Associates, Inc., Chicago, IL; photographs: Paul Schlismann, Deerfield, IL; pp. 150–151, design: Abramson Teiger Architects, Culver City, CA, and Wendi Anton, Anton Forster Interior Design, Culver City, CA; photographs: Peter Christiansen Valli, Los Angeles, CA; p. 152, design: Lash McDaniel, Scottsdale, AZ; photographs: © Mark Boisclair Photography, Inc., Phoenix, AZ; 154–155, design: Adolfo Perez, Architect, Newton, MA; photographs: Nick Wheeler, Weston, MA

CHAPTER ELEVEN. pp. 156–157, design: Cullman and Kravis, Inc., New York, NY, and Ira Grandberg & Associates, Mt. Kisco, NY; photographs: © Durston Saylor, New York, NY; p. 158, (left) design: M (Group), New York, NY; photograph: Dominique Vorillon, Los Angeles, CA; (right) design: Clodagh, New York, NY; photograph: © Daniel Aubry, New York, NY; p. 159, (left) design: Barbara Houston, M. Arch., B.E.S., Vancouver, B.C., Canada; photograph: Ed White Photographics, Vancouver, B.C., Canada; (right) design: Lash McDaniel, Scottsdale, AZ; photograph: © Mark Boisclair Photography, Inc., Phoenix, AZ; p. 160, (left) design: Sura Malaga-Strachan, Holmdel, NJ; photograph: Rosemary Carroll, Doylestown, PA; (right) design: Ken Zawislak, Royal Oak, MI, and Carol Grant, Royal Oak, MI; photograph: Beth Singer, Franklin, MI; p. 161, (left) design, Peter Sollogub, Chermayeff, Sollogub and Poole, Inc., Boston, MA, and Maho Abe, ZEN Associates Inc., Sudbury, MA; photograph: Richard Mandelkorn, Lincoln, MA; (right) design: M (Group), New York, NY; photograph: Dominique Vorillon, Los Angeles, CA; p. 162, (left) design: Gene Pindzia, Riverside Custom Design, Grosse Pointe, MI; photograph: Beth Singer, Franklin, MI; (right) design: Adolfo Perez, Architect, Newton, MA; photograph: Nick Wheeler, Weston, MA; p. 163, (left) design: Minsuk Cho and James Slade, Cho Slade Architecture, New York, NY; photograph: Jordi Miralles Sambola, Barcelona, Spain; (right) design: Erica Broberg Architect, East Hampton, NY; photograph: Tria Giovan, New York, NY; pp. 164–165, design: Donna Livingston Design, Los Angeles, CA; photographs: Mary E. Nichols, Los Angeles, CA; p. 166, design: Brininstool + Lynch, Chicago, IL; photographs: Christopher Barrett © Hedrich-Blessing, Chicago, IL; p. 167, design: Brininstool + Lynch, Chicago, IL; photograph: © Steve Richardson, Indianapolis, IN; pp. 168–169, design: Rosenblum Architects, New York, NY; photographs: © Durston Saylor, New York, NY; pp. 170–171, design: Clodagh, New York, NY; photograph: © Daniel Aubry, New York, NY

CHAPTER TWELVE. pp. 172–177, design: Cullman and Kravis, Inc., New York, NY, and Elliott Rosenblum, New York, NY; photographs: © Durston Saylor, New York, NY; pp. 178–179, design: Dujardin Design Associates, Westport, CT; photographs: © Durston Saylor, New York, NY; pp. 180–181, design: Mary Douglas Drysdale, Washington, D.C.; photographs: (p. 180 and 181 right) Andrew D. Lautman, Washington, D.C., (p. 181 left) Peter Vitale, Santa Fe, NM (© VERANDA Publications, Inc.); pp. 182–183, design: Abramson Teiger Architects, Culver City, CA; photographs: © John Linden, Woodland Hills, CA; pp. 184–185, design: Sandra Nunnerley Inc., New York, NY; photographs: Grant Mudford, Sydney, Australia; p. 186, design: Maxine Snider, Chicago, IL; photograph: Francois Robert, Tucson, AZ

index